CANNING & PRESERVING

GOOD
HOUSEKEEPING

CANNING & PRESERVING

80+ SIMPLE, SMALL-BATCH RECIPES

★ GOOD FOOD GUARANTEED ★

HEARST
books

HEARSTBOOKS

An Imprint of Sterling Publishing Co., Inc.
1166 Avenue of the Americas
New York, NY 10036

ISBN 978-1-61837-233-8

The Good Housekeeping Cookbook Seal guarantees that the recipes in this publication meet the strict standards
of the Good Housekeeping Research Institute. The Institute has been a source of reliable information and a consumer
advocate since 1900, and established its seal of approval in 1909. Every recipe in this publication has been
triple-tested for ease, reliability, and great taste by the Institute.

Hearst Communications, Inc. has made every effort to ensure that all information in this publication is accurate.
However, due to differing conditions, tools, and individual skills, Hearst Communications, Inc. cannot be responsible
for any injuries, losses and/or damages that may result from the use of any information in this publication.

Distributed in Canada by Sterling Publishing
c/o Canadian Manda Group, 664 Annette Street
Toronto, Ontario, M6S 2C8, Canada
Distributed in Australia by NewSouth Books
45 Beach Street, Coogee, NSW 2034, Australia

For information about custom editions, special sales, and premium and corporate purchases,
please contact Sterling Special Sales at 800-805-5489 or specialsales@sterlingpublishing.com.

Manufactured in China

2 4 6 8 10 9 7 5 3 1

goodhousekeeping.com
sterlingpublishing.com

Cover design by David Ter-Avanesyan
Interior design by Sharon Jacobs
For photography credits, see page 126

CONTENTS

Foreword

Canning jars have certainly proved that they are multitaskers. They're a Pinterest® phenomenon shown holding everything from flowers and cookie mixes to trifle and—their original use—preserved food. Yes, interest in canning and preserving is on the rise!

Seeing cases of canning jars stacked up at the local supermarket gets me plotting. What does your weekend look like? The canning process may seem a tad daunting at first, but it doesn't require any special equipment except patience. This is a method you can jump into for one hour or a few. If you're a first-timer, you may want to start with a batch of skillet jam or refrigerator pickles. Or you can set aside an entire morning and put up a batch of fresh-from-the-farm (or farmers' market) preserves.

Canning is all about preserving the flavors of the seasonal foods we love: local berries, tender cucumbers, ripe tomatoes, and so much more. You can capture the flavors of the harvest in a jam or mix things up with relishes, chutneys, and fruit butters. And we give you some recipes to use them in as well! I'm thrilled to share this collection of *Good Housekeeping* recipes with you.

Let this book be your essential guide to the kitchen craft. *Good Housekeeping Canning & Preserving* begins with a thorough introduction that highlights important equipment and procedures along with numerous triple-tested, small-batch recipes. These include healthful and homemade jams, jellies, chutneys, compotes, marmalades, pickles, and sauerkrauts, and they all pack huge flavor in small jars.

Whether you want to make a jam or chutney or savor summer veggies in tangy brine, these recipes will guide you in preserving the freshest flavors of the harvest. Now when I'm craving the taste of juicy summer strawberries, I can simply pop open a jar of preserves. Voilà—summer is served!

Looking for something sweet? Smear Peach-Honey Jam (page 21), Blushing Apple Butter (page 43), or Tangelo Marmalade (page 79) on a piece of toast. Want a little heat? Red Currant–Habanero Jelly (page 51), Spicy Rhubarb Chutney (page 72), and Spicy Pickled Green Beans (page 103) offer a punch. What about something unexpected to pair with cheese or meat? Try the Pickled Sour Cherries (page 115), Champagne & Grape Jelly (page 48), or Caramelized Onion & Bacon Jam (page 26).

Along with essential canning recipes, we've included these sweet and savory components in everyday cooking. Peach Jam–Glazed Chicken (page 23) gives new life to a classic baked dish. Beef Tenderloin with Citrus–Red Pepper Chutney (page 74) makes for a great holiday meal. Cantaloupe Jam is the perfect condiment for a Prosciutto-Melon Panini (page 18). And Cherry Linzer Bars (page 37) are even more special when you make the jam, too.

So what are you waiting for? Check out what looks good in your market and whip up a batch of seasonal favorites. Happy canning!

SUSAN WESTMORELAND
Food Director, *Good Housekeeping*

Introduction

Today, most people process fruits and vegetables because they enjoy it, not because they have to. The fruits and vegetables for homemade pickles, jams, preserves, and jellies can come from an urban farmers' market or the garden out back. Canning and preserving offer satisfying pleasures. Nothing produced commercially equals the quality or flavor.

Equipment for Canning Fruits & Tomatoes

BOILING-WATER-BATH CANNING POT

If you plan on doing a lot of canning, you may want to purchase a canning pot. It comes with a basket to hold the jars and a tight-fitting lid. However, any large stockpot will do, as long as it is deep enough that the pot's rim is 3 to 4 inches above the tops of the jars (as they sit on the wire basket or rack) and large enough that the jars don't touch each other. Instead of a wire canning basket, you can use any sturdy heatproof rack that will fit in the pot; round wire cooling racks work well. If your improvised rack needs a little extra support to hold heavy jars, place several metal jar bands underneath the center of the rack.

JARS Tempered glass canning jars, sometimes called Mason jars, are the only recommended jars for home canning. Their special two-piece lids ensure a vacuum-tight seal that discourages spoilage. Also, the specially treated glass will keep them from cracking when they're subjected to extreme temperatures. If you plan to put your jars in the freezer, buy the ones with straight

or tapered sides; jars with "shoulders" don't work in the freezer. Jars range in size. Use the size recommended in the recipe, especially for hot-water-bath canning; if you use larger jars than recommended, the heat that kills harmful microorganisms may not penetrate all the way through the food, or preserves may not set up properly. Wide-mouthed jars are easier to fill than narrow ones. The jars are reusable, but check them carefully beforehand for any signs of wear, like cracks or chips.

CAPS The most common cap is made of two pieces: a flat lid with a rubberlike sealing compound on the underside and a metal screw band that holds the lid in place during processing. The lids are not reusable. Undamaged screw bands, however, can be reused.

UTENSILS FOR CANNING A wide-mouthed funnel for transferring the food to the jars and a jar lifter to grip them from the boiling water aren't essential but helpful. To remove air bubbles, use a narrow rubber spatula.

Canning Steps

For best results, read these steps thoroughly before you begin.

• **Prepare jars and lids for processing.** Check the jars to be sure there are no chips or cracks. Wash the jars, lids, and screw bands in hot soapy water; rinse. The jars must be heated before canning to prevent breakage. Submerge them in enough cool water to cover; then heat water to boiling. Remove the pot from the heat and cover it. Leave the jars in the hot water for at least 10 minutes. Place the lids and bands in a saucepan with enough water to cover; bring to a simmer (180°F). Remove the pan from the heat, cover it, and keep hot until ready to use. Remove the jars and lids, one at a time, as needed.

• **Prep fruit/tomatoes and pack jars.** Fruit and tomatoes can be packed into the hot jars raw (cold pack) or slightly cooked (hot pack). In both methods, the fruit is covered with boiling hot liquid—water, juice, or sugar syrup. See the chart on pages 12-13 for the best methods for the fruit you intend to can.

• **Cold pack.** Firmly pack the unheated raw fruit into hot jars, then fill with boiling liquid to within ½ inch of the rim. You will need ½ to 1½ cups of liquid for every 4 cups of fruit.

• **Hot pack.** Cooking makes food more pliable and easier to pack, so you will need fewer jars. Pack the hot food loosely into hot jars and fill with boiling liquid to within ½ inch of the rim.

• **For both cold and hot pack.** (Headspace is important: if a jar has too little, the food may swell and force itself under the lid, breaking the seal.) Too much headspace and the food at the top of the jar could discolor. After filling each jar, with cold or hot food, run a narrow rubber spatula between the food and the side of the jar to remove any air bubbles. Using a clean, damp cloth, thoroughly wipe the jar rims and threads to remove any drips of food or liquid. Cover with the hot lids. Screw on the bands just until tightened; do not force.

• **Process jars.** The filled jars must be processed in a boiling-water bath immediately after packing to maintain the proper temperature. The processing time will vary according to the type of fruit, the method of packing, and the size of the jars. Place the basket or a rack in the canning pot. Fill the pot halfway with hot water; heat it to simmering over High heat. In another pot or kettle, heat additional water to boiling. Carefully place the filled jars in the basket far enough apart so the water can circulate freely around them. The water level should be 1 to 2 inches above the tops of the jars; add boiling water if needed. Cover the canner and heat the water to boiling. Start timing as soon as the water comes to a full boil; check often. Reduce the heat to maintain a gentle boil for the time indicated in the recipe. If necessary, add boiling water to keep the jars properly covered. Once you've processed the jars for the required time, turn off the heat, remove the lid, and let the jars sit in the hot water for 5 minutes.

• **Cool jars.** In a draft-free place, line the counter surface with folded kitchen towels (contact with a cold, hard surface could break the jars). With a jar lifter, remove the jars from the pot and place them on the towels, allowing 1 to 2 inches between them for air circulation. (If any liquid has boiled out of the jars, do not open them to add more.) Cool to room temperature, at least 12 hours or up to 24 hours.

• **Test jars for airtight seal.** When the jars are cool, check the seals. The lids should be slightly concave (indented), not flat or bulging. If you hit the top of the lid of a properly sealed jar with a teaspoon, you will be rewarded with a high-pitched ringing sound. If you get a dull thud, you don't have a proper seal. Any food in a jar that hasn't sealed properly needs to be refrigerated and eaten within several days or reheated and processed in a newly sterilized jar with a new lid.

• **Store jars properly.** Wipe the jars with a clean, damp cloth to remove any food residue and label them, including the date of processing. Store the jars in a cool, dark place, preferably between 50°F and 70°F. Under ideal conditions, home-processed foods will keep for about a year; after that, changes in the flavor, color, and texture will affect the quality.

Making Jams, Jellies & Other Fruit Spreads

If you have a large quantity of fruit, make a big batch of jam. And remember, you don't always have to pull out the canning pot for water-bath processing. Excellent jams can be prepared for storage right in your freezer.

You'll need the same equipment as for canning fruit, with the addition of a broad 8-quart Dutch oven for preparing large-batch recipes and a 12-inch skillet for small-batch skillet jams. Don't use unlined aluminum pots or skillets, as they can react with the acid in fruit and affect the flavor and color.

When preparing the fruit, don't puree it: if you do, it won't set. Cook as directed. Some recipes use commercial pectin to set mixtures

Keeping Fruit Color Bright

Some fruit will turn brown if left untreated after it's been cut or peeled. Whether canning or freezing, you can keep fruit color bright by treating it. **SOAKING METHOD:** In a large bowl, combine 4 quarts water, 2 tablespoons salt, and 2 tablespoons cider or white vinegar. As the fruit is peeled or cut, drop it into the solution. Let stand a few minutes, then remove, rinse well, and drain. **ASCORBIC ACID:** Available in supermarkets, ascorbic acid can be added to the sugar syrup or mixed with a little water and sprinkled over the fruit.

properly. Pectin is a naturally occurring substance found in varying amounts in fruits; underripe fruit contains more pectin than fully ripe fruit. Commercial pectin comes in powdered and liquid forms: they are not interchangeable.

If the recipe calls for the fruit to come to a "rolling boil," heat it until the mixture forms bubbles across its surface that cannot be stirred down. Skim off foam. To do this, remove the pan from the heat. Use a large metal spoon to skim the surface.

Once you've cooked the jam, jelly, or fruit spread as directed, spoon it into hot jars prepared as instructed on page 9. For freezer jams, pack the jam into containers to ½ inch from the tops; cover tightly. Freeze. For processed spreads, preferably using a wide-mouthed funnel, fill and close the jars one at a time. For jellies, fill the jars to ⅛ inch from the tops; for jams, ¼ inch from the tops. Wipe the rims of the jars with a clean, damp cloth. Place the lids on top, then screw on the bands. Process, cool, test, and store the jars as instructed on pages 9–10.

Skillet Jams

Prepare jars and lids (page 9). If using blackberries and/or raspberries, press 1/2 cup crushed berries through a sieve to remove seeds. In a heavy nonstick skillet, combine desired fruit and indicated amount of pectin and butter. Heat to boiling over High heat, stirring constantly. Stir in sugar and heat to boiling, stirring constantly; boil 1 minute or, for apricots, boil until softened, 2 to 3 minutes. Remove skillet from heat. Quickly ladle hot jam into hot jars. Wipe jar rims and threads clean; cover with lids. Refrigerate until set, about 6 hours. Refrigerate up to 3 weeks. Each recipe makes two 8-ounce jars.

JAM	FRUIT MIXTURE	BUTTER OR MARGARINE	FRUIT PECTIN	POWDERED SUGAR
Apricot Skillet Jam	1 pound apricots, pitted and finely chopped, tossed with 2 teaspoons fresh lemon juice	2 tablespoons	none	1 cup
Blueberry Skillet Jam	2 cups blueberries, crushed	2 tablespoons	½ teaspoon	1 cup
Raspberry Skillet Jam	3 cups raspberries, crushed	4 teaspoons	½ teaspoon	1½ cups
Strawberry Skillet Jam	2 cups sliced strawberries, crushed	4 teaspoons	½ teaspoon	1 cup
Three-Berry Skillet Jam	1 cup each blackberries, raspberries, and sliced strawberries, crushed	4 teaspoons	½ teaspoon	1 cup
Peach Skillet Jam	1 pound peaches, peeled, pitted, and mashed with 2 teaspoons fresh lemon juice	2 tablespoons	½ teaspoon	1 cup

Canning Fruits & Tomatoes in a Boiling-Water Bath*

HOW TO PREPARE	HOW TO PACK	PROCESSING
Apricots Peel apricots, if you like. To peel, plunge fruit into boiling water for 30 seconds; transfer to cold water to help loosen skins. Cut in half; remove pits. Slice, if desired. Treat to prevent darkening (page 10).	**HOT PACK:** Heat apricots in water, juice, or light or medium syrup to boiling. Pack fruit in hot jars in layers. Cover with boiling liquid; leave ½-inch headspace. Adjust caps.	20 min/pint 25 min/quart
Berries Wash berries; drain. Remove stems. (Use sugar syrup appropriate for sweetness of your berries.)	**COLD PACK:** Pack berries in hot jars; gently shake to pack tightly. Cover with boiling water, juice, or syrup; leave ½-inch headspace. Adjust caps. **HOT PACK:** Cook berries in boiling water for 30 seconds; drain. Pack in hot jars. Cover with boiling liquid; leave ½-inch headspace. Adjust caps.	15 min/pint 20 min/quart 15 min/pint 15 min/quart
Cherries Rinse, then remove stems; pit, if desired. If pitted, treat to prevent darkening (page 10.) If unpitted, prick cherries to prevent splitting.	**COLD PACK:** Pour ½ cup boiling water, juice, or light or medium sugar syrup for sweet cherries or medium or heavy sugar syrup for sour cherries into each hot jar. Fill jar with cherries; shake to pack down. Cover with boiling liquid; leave ½-inch headspace. Adjust caps. **HOT PACK:** In saucepot, add ½ cup liquid for each 4 cups cherries. Cover; heat to boiling, then pack cherries in hot jars. Cover with boiling liquid; leave ½-inch headspace. Adjust caps.	25 min/pint 25 min/quart 15 min/pint 20 min/quart
Figs Rinse; drain. In saucepot, cover figs with water and heat to boiling; boil 2 minutes. Drain.	**HOT PACK:** In saucepot, in light syrup, heat figs to boiling; boil 5 minutes. Add bottled lemon juice per Tomatoes, opposite page. Pack hot jars with figs. Cover with boiling syrup; leave ½-inch headspace. Adjust caps.	45 min/pint 50 min/quart

These boiling times are based on an altitude of 1 to 1,000 feet above sea level.

HOW TO PREPARE	HOW TO PACK	PROCESSING
Peaches Peel peaches (see Apricots, opposite page); cut in half. Remove pits. Scrape red fibers from cavities. Slice, if desired. Treat to prevent darkening (page 10).	**HOT PACK:** Heat peaches in water, juice, or medium or heavy syrup to boiling, then pack as for Apricots, in layers, cut side down.	20 min/pint 25 min/quart
Pears Cut pears in half or into quarters; core and peel. Treat to prevent darkening (page 10).	**HOT PACK:** In saucepot, in water, juice, or light or medium syrup, heat pears to boiling; boil 5 minutes. Pack in hot jars. Cover with boiling liquid; leave ½-inch headspace. Adjust caps.	20 min/pint 25 min/quart
Plums Use firm, meaty varieties, not very juicy ones. Wash; prick skins if left whole to prevent bursting. For Italian prune plums and other freestone varieties, cut in half and remove pits, if desired.	**HOT PACK:** In saucepot, in water or medium syrup, heat plums to boiling; boil 2 minutes. Remove pot from heat. Cover; let stand 20 to 30 minutes. Pack plums in hot jars. Cover with boiling liquid; leave ½-inch headspace. Adjust caps.	20 min/pint 25 min/quart
Rhubarb, stewed Cut stewed rhubarb stalks into ½-inch to 1-inch pieces.	**HOT PACK:** In saucepot, combine ½ cup sugar for each 4 cups rhubarb; mix well. Let stand until juices appear. Heat mixture to boiling. Immediately pack in hot jars; leave ½-inch headspace (add boiling water to cover). Adjust caps.	15 min/pint 15 min/quart
Tomatoes Use only firm-ripe—not overripe—tomatoes (as they lose their acidity). Plunge into boilinwwg water 30 seconds to loosen skins. Transfer to cold water; drain. Peel and cut out stem ends. Leave whole or cut in half or into quarters for cold pack; quarter for crushed tomatoes (hot pack).	**COLD PACK:** To each quart jar, add 2 tablespoons bottled lemon juice; to each pint jar, add 1 tablespoon. Add salt, if desired, 1 teaspoon per quart or ½ teaspoon per pint. Pack hot jars with raw tomatoes, pressing down untill all the spaces are filled with juices. Leave ½-inch headspace. Adjust caps. **HOT PACK:** In saucepot, crush one quarter of the tomatoes with a wooden spoon. Heat crushed tomatoes to boiling, stirring. Add remaining tomatoes and heat to boiling; boil 5 minutes. Add lemon juice and salt. Pack in jars per cold pack, above. Adjust caps.	85 min/pint 85 min/quart 35 min/pint 45 min/quart

* These boiling times are based on an altitude of 1 to 1,000 feet above sea level.

*Tomato-Black Pepper Jam (page 20),
Peach & Honey Jam (page 21), and
Raspberry Skillet Jam (page 38)*

1 Jams & Preserves

Nothing beats a piece of buttery toast with sweet jam smeared on top. And although that is the traditional way to savor jams and preserves, there are plenty of other options, too. In this chapter, we provide recipes for classics, like Mixed Berry Jam, and offer flavor twists as well, like Apple, Strawberry & Mint Jam. Vanilla-Nectarine Jam or Tomato–Black Pepper Jam can be spread on top of avocado toast, and Cantaloupe Jam can add a sweet touch to a panini. We also offer recipes that incorporate your homemade preserves, like PB&J Bars or Peach Jam–Glazed Chicken.

BONUS RECIPES

Berry-Stuffed Cupcakes (*page 17*), **Prosciutto-Melon Panini** (*page 18*), **Peppery Avocado Toast** (*page 20*), **Peach Shortcakes** (*page 21*), **Peach Jam–Glazed Chicken** (*page 23*), **Turkey Meat Loaf with Tomato Jam** (*page 25*), **Jammy Thumbprints** (*page 30*), **PB&J Bars** (*page 31*), **Cherry Linzer Bars** (*page 37*)

Apple, Strawberry & Mint JAM

ACTIVE TIME: 25 MINUTES   **TOTAL TIME:** 40 MINUTES   **MAKES:** 7 (8-OUNCE) JARS

- 2 pounds fresh strawberries
- 2 teaspoons lemon zest
- 2 tablespoons lemon juice
- 2 cups superfine sugar
- 2 Granny Smith apples
- ¼ cup fresh mint
- 3 tablespoons instant pectin (such as Ball® RealFruit™ instant pectin)

1 In a bowl, toss together strawberries, lemon zest, juice, and ¼ cup sugar. Fold in apples and mint, and let sit for 15 minutes.

2 In a bowl, whisk together 1¾ cups sugar and pectin. Sprinkle the mixture over the fruit, then stir constantly for 2 minutes. Using a potato masher, lightly crush the mixture for 1 minute.

3 Transfer to 8-ounce freezer-safe jars (about ¾ cup per jar), leaving a ½-inch space at the top of each jar.

4 Refrigerate for at least 3 days before serving, or freeze for up to 1 year. Thaw in the fridge overnight (once open, consume within 1 week).

EACH SERVING (1 TABLESPOON): ABOUT 25 CALORIES, 0G PROTEIN, 6G CARBOHYDRATE, 0G FAT, (0G SATURATED), 0G FIBER, 5MG SODIUM

Blueberry, Orange & Lime JAM

ACTIVE TIME: 15 MINUTES   **TOTAL TIME:** 35 MINUTES   **MAKES:** 6 (8-OUNCE) JARS

- 2 teaspoons orange zest
- 2 navel oranges, peeled and chopped
- 2 pounds fresh blueberries
- 2 teaspoons lime zest
- 2 tablespoons fresh lime juice
- 1 cup superfine sugar
- 3 tablespoons instant pectin (such as Ball RealFruit instant pectin)

1 In a bowl, toss together orange zest, oranges, blueberries, lime zest and juice, and ¼ cup sugar.

2 Using a potato masher, lightly crush the fruit mixture and let sit for 15 minutes.

3 Whisk together ¾ cup sugar and pectin. Sprinkle over the mixture, then stir constantly for 2 minutes.

4 Transfer to 8-ounce freezer-safe jars (about ¼ cup per jar), leaving a ½ inch space at the top of each jar.

5 Refrigerate for at least 3 days before serving, or freeze for up to 1 year. Thaw in the fridge overnight (once open, consume within 1 week).

EACH SERVING (1 TABLESPOON): ABOUT 20 CALORIES, 0G PROTEIN, 5G CARBOHYDRATE, 0G FAT, (0G SATURATED), 0G FIBER, 5MG SODIUM

Mixed Berry
JAM

ACTIVE TIME: 15 MINUTES   **TOTAL TIME:** 35 MINUTES, PLUS COOLING   **MAKES:** 2½ CUPS

3   cups mixed fresh raspberries, blueberries, and blackberries

3   tablespoons lemon juice

1   tablespoon powdered no- or low-sugar pectin

½   cup sugar

⅓   cup honey

1 In a food processor, pulse berries until finely chopped, stopping and stirring occasionally.

2 In a 4-quart saucepan, combine the berries, ⅔ cup water, and lemon juice; stir in pectin. Heat on High to a vigorous boil that cannot be stirred down, stirring frequently. Stir in sugar and honey. Return to a vigorous boil that cannot be stirred down, stirring constantly. Boil for 1 minute. Remove from the heat.

3 Transfer to heatproof jars or containers. Let cool at room temperature. Cover and refrigerate overnight or until set. Keep in the refrigerator for up to 1 month.

EACH SERVING (1 TABLESPOON): ABOUT 25 CALORIES, 0G PROTEIN, 6G CARBOHYDRATE, 0G FAT (0G SATURATED), 0G FIBER, 1MG SODIUM

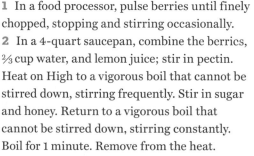

Berry-Stuffed Cupcakes

With a paring knife held at an angle, cut the centers from the tops of 24 vanilla cupcakes. Fill each hole with **1 teaspoon Mixed Berry Jam**. Stir **1 tablespoon jam** into **2½ cups vanilla frosting**. Spoon the frosting into a piping bag fitted with a pastry tip. Pipe the icing onto the cupcakes. Serves 24.

EACH SERVING (1 CUPCAKE): ABOUT 320 CALORIES, 3G PROTEIN, 47G CARBOHYDRATE, 13G FAT (7G SATURATED), 1G FIBER, 187MG SODIUM

Cantaloupe
JAM

Sweet melon jam makes a stellar toast topper.

ACTIVE TIME: 15 MINUTES **TOTAL TIME:** 35 MINUTES, PLUS COOLING **MAKES:** 3 CUPS

3   cups coarsely chopped ripe cantaloupe

3   tablespoons lemon juice

2   tablespoons powdered no- or low-sugar pectin

½   cup sugar

⅓   cup honey

1 In a food processor, pulse the cantaloupe until finely chopped, stopping and stirring occasionally.

2 In a 4-quart saucepan, combine cantaloupe, ⅔ cup water, and lemon juice; stir in pectin. Heat on High to a vigorous boil that cannot be stirred down, stirring frequently. Stir in sugar and honey. Return to a vigorous boil that cannot be stirred down, stirring constantly. Boil for 3 minutes. Remove from the heat.

3 Transfer to heatproof jars or containers. Let cool at room temperature. Cover and refrigerate overnight or until set. Keep in the refrigerator for up to 1 month.

EACH SERVING (1 TABLESPOON): ABOUT 20 CALORIES, 0G PROTEIN, 5G CARBOHYDRATE, 0G FAT (0G SATURATED), 0G FIBER, 3MG SODIUM

Prosciutto-Melon Panini

Preheat your oven to 450°F. Cut a **ciabatta roll** in half and spread **2 tablespoons Cantaloupe Jam** on the bottom half. Next, layer **4 thin slices mozzarella**, **4 slices prosciutto**, and a **handful of arugula**. Replace the top of the roll. Bake in the oven until the cheese melts. Serves 1.

EACH SERVING: ABOUT 630 CALORIES, 47G PROTEIN, 54G CARBOHYDRATE, 26G FAT (14G SATURATED), 2G FIBER, 2,238MG SODIUM

TIP

Pectin is a natural, fruit-based ingredient used to thicken jams and jellies. For best results, we suggest using Ball RealFruit Low or No-Sugar Needed Pectin.

Tomato–Black Pepper
JAM

Amp up a cheese platter with this savory homemade jam.

ACTIVE TIME: 15 MINUTES · **TOTAL TIME:** 35 MINUTES, PLUS COOLING · **MAKES:** 4 CUPS

4	cups (about 5 medium) ripe tomatoes, coarsely chopped
2	tablespoons lemon juice
1	tablespoon powdered no- or low-sugar pectin
½	cup sugar
⅓	cup honey

kosher salt

ground black pepper

1 In a food processor, pulse the tomatoes until finely chopped, stopping and stirring occasionally.

2 In a 4-quart saucepan, combine the tomatoes, ⅓ cup water, and lemon juice; stir in pectin. Heat on High to a vigorous boil that cannot be stirred down, stirring frequently. Stir in sugar and honey. Return to a vigorous boil that cannot be stirred down, stirring constantly. Boil for 1 minute. Remove from the heat.

3 Stir in ¼ teaspoon salt and ½ teaspoon pepper. Transfer to heatproof jars or containers. Let cool at room temperature. Cover and refrigerate overnight or until set. Keep in the refrigerator for up to 1 month.

EACH SERVING (1 TABLESPOON): ABOUT 15 CALORIES, 0G PROTEIN, 4G CARBOHYDRATE, 0G FAT (0G SATURATED), 0G FIBER, 9MG SODIUM

Peppery Avocado Toast

Mash **½ small ripe avocado** with **½ teaspoon lime juice** and **⅛ teaspoon salt**. Toast **1 large slice whole-wheat sourdough bread**. Spread the avocado mash on the toast. Top with **1 tablespoon Tomato–Black Pepper Jam**. Serves 1.

EACH SERVING: ABOUT 290 CALORIES, 6G PROTEIN, 31G CARBOHYDRATE, 16G FAT (2G SATURATED), 9G FIBER, 449MG SODIUM

Peach & Honey
JAM

Preserve ripe summer peaches in an easy, homemade jam.

ACTIVE TIME: 15 MINUTES   **TOTAL TIME:** 35 MINUTES, PLUS COOLING   **MAKES:** 2¹/₂ CUPS

3   cups coarsely chopped, peeled ripe peaches (about 5 medium)

3   tablespoons lemon juice

1   tablespoon powdered no- or low-sugar pectin

¹/₂   cup sugar

¹/₃   cup honey

1 In a food processor, pulse peaches until finely chopped, stopping and stirring occasionally.

2 In a 4-quart saucepan, combine peaches, ²/₃ cup water, and lemon juice; stir in pectin. Heat on High to a vigorous boil that cannot be stirred down, stirring frequently. Stir in sugar and honey. Return to a vigorous boil that cannot be stirred down, stirring constantly. Boil for 1 minute. Remove from the heat.

3 Transfer to heatproof jars or containers. Let cool at room temperature. Cover and refrigerate overnight or until set. Keep in the refrigerator for up to 1 month.

EACH SERVING (1 TABLESPOON): ABOUT 25 CALORIES, 0G PROTEIN, 7G CARBOHYDRATE, 0G FAT (0G SATURATED), 0G FIBER, 1MG SODIUM

Peach Shortcakes

Split **8 homemade** or **store-bought biscuits.** Fill each with **3 tablespoons whipped cream.** Top each with **1 tablespoon Peach & Honey Jam.** Serves 8.

ONE SHORTCAKE: ABOUT 225 CALORIES, 4G PROTEIN, 36G CARBOHYDRATE, 8G FAT (2G SATURATED), 1G FIBER, 482MG SODIUM

 TIP

Stir in 1 tablespoon hot pepper sauce along with sugar to add a little Southern sass.

Peach Jam–Glazed
CHICKEN

This sweet-and-savory glaze adds new flavor to classic baked chicken.

ACTIVE TIME: 10 MINUTES **TOTAL TIME:** 1 HOUR AND 10 MINUTES **MAKES:** 4 SERVINGS

1   chicken (or 2 bone-in split chicken breasts)

sea salt

freshly ground pepper

juice of 1 lemon

¾   cup Peach & Honey jam (prepared or page 21)

4   garlic cloves, crushed

1 Preheat your oven to 400°F. Place chicken pieces in a 10-inch, oven-safe skillet or a 10 x 8-inch baking dish. Season with 1 teaspoon salt and ½ teaspoon pepper and squeeze lemon juice over the chicken. Stir the jam and garlic together and spread over the chicken.

2 Bake uncovered until juices run clear and meat reaches 165°F, about 1 hour.

EACH SERVING: ABOUT 475 CALORIES, 45G PROTEIN, 23G CARBOHYDRATE, 22G FAT (6G SATURATED), 1G FIBER, 617MG SODIUM

23

Turkey Meat Loaf
WITH TOMATO JAM

The spicy tomato jam that tops the finished meat loaf
is a sophisticated and chunky twist on ketchup.

ACTIVE TIME: 25 MINUTES   **TOTAL TIME:** 1 HOUR 30 MINUTES   **MAKES:** 8 SERVINGS

TURKEY MEATLOAF

olive oil

½ pound shiitake mushrooms

salt

ground black pepper

2¼ teaspoons finely chopped fresh
thyme leaves

3 tablespoons diced roasted red peppers

2 pounds ground turkey (1 pound each,
white and dark meat)

1½ cups bread crumbs

2 garlic cloves, crushed

1 tablespoon chopped fresh sage leaves

1 teaspoon ground ginger

1 medium onion, chopped

TOMATO JAM

2 (28-ounce) cans diced fire-roasted tomatoes

1 teaspoon crushed red pepper

2 tablespoons balsamic vinegar

½ cup light brown sugar

¼ teaspoon allspice

1 To prepare the Meat Loaf: Preheat oven to
350°F. In a nonstick skillet over Medium-High
heat, heat 1 tablespoon oil. Sauté mushrooms
until beginning to brown, about 6 minutes.

Season with ½ teaspoon each salt and pepper and
¼ teaspoon thyme. Brown mushrooms, stirring,
about 6 minutes. Stir in red peppers. Transfer
mixture to a plate and let cool.

2 Meanwhile, in a large bowl, mix turkey, bread
crumbs, garlic, sage, ginger, half the onion, and
¼ teaspoon salt and 2 teaspoons thyme. Using
your hands, pack half the turkey mixture into a
9 x 5-inch loaf pan greased with 1 teaspoon oil.
Top with an even layer of mushroom mixture.
Cover with remaining turkey and pat down.
Bake for 40 minutes.

3 To prepare the Jam: Meanwhile, in a large
skillet over Medium heat, heat 2 tablespoons oil
and cook remaining onion until softened, about
8 minutes. Add tomatoes, crushed red pepper,
vinegar, brown sugar, and allspice; simmer over
Medium heat for 30 minutes.

4 Remove meat loaf from oven and spread ¾
cup tomato jam on top. Return to oven and bake
until meat loaf reaches 165°F on an instant-read
thermometer, about 30 minutes more. Let cool in
pan, about 10 minutes. Turn out and slice. Serve
with the remaining tomato jam on the side.

EACH SERVING: ABOUT 375 CALORIES, 29G PROTEIN,
38G CARBOHYDRATE, 12G FAT (3G SATURATED),
3G FIBER, 661MG SODIUM

CARAMELIZED
Onion & Bacon Jam

Spread this smoky jam on baguette slices with goat cheese for hors d'oeuvres, or spread a couple tablespoons under the skin of a chicken before roasting.

ACTIVE TIME: 20 MINUTES   **TOTAL TIME:** 1 HOUR AND 50 MINUTES   **MAKES:** 3 CUPS

1½ pounds bacon, finely chopped

3   large onions, finely chopped

1   medium leek, finely chopped

2   garlic cloves, finely chopped

salt

½   cup balsamic vinegar

½   cup packed brown sugar

½   teaspoon dried oregano

¼   teaspoon ground nutmeg

ground black pepper

1 In a deep 12-inch skillet, cook bacon on Medium heat for 30 minutes or until crisp and fat has rendered, stirring occasionally. With a slotted spoon, transfer the bacon to a paper towel–lined plate. Remove and discard all but 2 tablespoons of the bacon fat in the skillet.

2 To the fat in the skillet, add onions, leek, garlic, and ¼ teaspoon salt. Cook on Medium for 50 minutes or until caramelized and soft, stirring occasionally. Add vinegar, brown sugar, oregano, nutmeg, bacon, and ½ teaspoon pepper. Cook for 15 minutes or until onions are very soft.

3 Transfer the mixture to a food processor; pulse until finely chopped. Transfer to 4 small jars; refrigerate until cold. Jam may be refrigerated for up to 2 weeks.

EACH SERVING (1 TABLESPOON): ABOUT 45 CALORIES, 2G PROTEIN, 4G CARBOHYDRATES, 3G FAT (1G SATURATED), 95MG SODIUM

FREEZER
Strawberry Jam

Jewel-like freezer jam is especially fresh-tasting.
Peak-of-the-season farm stand strawberries work best.

ACTIVE TIME: 35 MINUTES **TOTAL TIME:** 35 MINUTES, PLUS OVERNIGHT TO STAND
MAKES: 5 (8-OUNCE) CONTAINERS

1   quart fully ripe strawberries, hulled

4   cups sugar

2   tablespoons fresh lemon juice

1   (1¾-ounce) package powdered fruit pectin

1 Prepare 5 (8-ounce) freezer-safe containers
with tight-fitting lids (page 9).
2 In a large bowl, thoroughly crush enough
strawberries to fill 2 cups. Stir in sugar and
lemon juice until thoroughly mixed; let stand
for 10 minutes.
3 In a 1-quart saucepan, combine ¾ cup water
and pectin and heat to boiling over High heat.
Boil, stirring constantly, for 1 minute. Stir pectin
mixture into fruit until sugar has dissolved and
mixture is no longer grainy, 3 to 4 minutes.
A few sugar crystals will remain.
4 Quickly ladle the jam into the containers to
within ½ inch of the tops. Wipe the container
rims clean; cover with the lids.
5 Let stand at room temperature until set, about
24 hours. Refrigerate for up to 3 weeks, or freeze
for up to 1 year. To use, place the frozen jam in
the refrigerator until thawed, about 4 hours.

EACH SERVING (1 TABLESPOON): ABOUT 40 CALORIES,
0G PROTEIN, 11G CARBOHYDRATE, 0G TOTAL FAT
(0G SATURATED), 1MG SODIUM

Freezer Raspberry Jam

For this quick way to prepare ruby-red
raspberry jam, thoroughly crush **1 quart fully
ripe raspberries** instead of strawberries, as
directed. If you like, press half the crushed
berries through a sieve and into a bowl to
remove the seeds; discard the seeds. Combine
with remaining **crushed berries**. Stir in **2 cups
sugar** until thoroughly mixed; let stand for
10 minutes.

Substitute **1 (3-ounce) pouch liquid fruit
pectin** for powdered pectin. In a small bowl,
combine pectin and lemon juice. Stir the pectin
mixture into fruit until sugar has dissolved
and continue with recipe as directed. Makes
four (8-ounce) freezer-safe containers of jam.

EACH SERVING (1 TABLESPOON): ABOUT 50 CALORIES,
0G PROTEIN, 13G CARBOHYDRATE, 0G TOTAL FAT
(0G SATURATED), 0MG SODIUM

Jammy
THUMBPRINTS

Chilling the cookie dough before baking solidifies the fat in the dough, making sure your cookies have a chewy yet crisp texture.

ACTIVE TIME: 35 MINUTES   **TOTAL TIME:** 55 MINUTES   **MAKES:** ABOUT 48 COOKIES

2¼ cups all-purpose flour

1 teaspoon baking powder

½ teaspoon baking soda

¾ cup butter or margarine

¾ cup sugar

salt

1 large egg yolk

2 tablespoons light corn syrup

1½ teaspoons vanilla extract

½ teaspoon almond extract

¼ cup walnuts or pecans

Freezer Raspberry Jam (prepared or page 28)

1 Preheat your oven to 375°F. Line a large cookie sheet with parchment paper.

2 In a medium bowl, whisk flour, baking powder, and baking soda; set aside. With a mixer on Medium-High speed, beat butter, sugar, and ½ teaspoon salt until creamy; beat in egg yolk, corn syrup, and extracts. With the mixer on Medium-Low speed, beat in the flour mixture until just combined.

3 Roll the dough into ½-inch balls, then roll the balls in chopped walnuts or pecans.

4 Place on a large cookie sheet, 2 inches apart. With the end of wooden spoon handle, make a deep indentation in each ball. Place the cookie sheet into the freezer for 30 minutes. After freezing but before baking, add ½ teaspoon apricot jam or Freezer Raspberry Jam (page 28) to each indentation.

5 Bake for 10 to 12 minutes or until golden around the edges. Let cool on the baking sheets for 5 minutes before transferring onto a wire rack; cool completely.

EACH SERVING (1 COOKIE): ABOUT 75 CALORIES, 1G PROTEIN, 11G CARBOHYDRATE, 3G FAT (2G SATURATED), 0G FIBER, 70MG SODIUM

TIP

Total time does not include freezing the cookies.

PB&J
BARS

Take your love of peanut butter and jelly to the next level with these easy and delicious bar cookies.

ACTIVE TIME: 15 MINUTES   **TOTAL TIME:** 45 MINUTES   **MAKES:** ABOUT 42 BARS

nonstick cooking spray

¾ cup (1½ sticks) butter or margarine, softened

½ cup packed brown sugar

salt

1 large egg

1½ teaspoons vanilla extract

2 cups all-purpose flour

¾ cup Freezer Strawberry Jam (prepared or page 28)

¾ cup peanut butter chips

1 Preheat your oven to 375°F. Line a 13 x 9-inch baking pan with foil, extending over the rim. Spray the foil with nonstick baking spray.

2 In a large bowl with a mixer on Medium-High speed, beat butter, brown sugar, and ½ teaspoon salt until light and fluffy. Beat in egg and vanilla. Reduce the speed to low; gradually beat in flour just until blended, occasionally scraping the bowl with a rubber spatula. Transfer to the prepared pan. With lightly floured hands, spread the dough into an even layer.

3 Bake 25 to 30 minutes or until deep golden brown around edges. Cool for about 10 minutes. Spread the warm crust with Freezer Strawberry Jam (page 28); top evenly with peanut butter chips. Cool completely in the pan on a wire rack.

4 Using the foil, remove the bar from the pan. Cut into 1-inch squares.

EACH SERVING (1 BAR): ABOUT 95 CALORIES, 1G PROTEIN, 12G CARBOHYDRATE, 4G FAT (3G SATURATED), 0G FIBER, 60MG SODIUM

Plum, Ginger & Lemon
JAM

The three distinct flavors in the jam meld together to make
a deliciously distinctive and satisfying spread.

ACTIVE TIME: 20 MINUTES   **TOTAL TIME:** 35 MINUTES   **MAKES:** 7 (8-OUNCE) JARS

3   pounds red plums

2   teaspoons lemon zest

2   tablespoons lemon juice

1   piece fresh ginger

2   cups superfine sugar

3   tablespoons instant pectin (such as Ball RealFruit instant pectin)

1 In a large bowl, toss together plums, lemon zest, juice, and ginger.

2 In a medium bowl, whisk together sugar and pectin. Sprinkle the sugar mixture over the fruit, then fold and stir constantly for 2 minutes. Using a potato masher, lightly crush the fruit mixture for 1 minute.

3 Transfer to 8-ounce freezer-safe jars (about ¾ cup per jar), leaving a ½ inch of space at the top of each jar.

4 Refrigerate for at least 3 days before serving, or freeze for up to 1 year. If frozen, thaw in the refrigerator overnight before serving (once open, consume within 1 week).

EACH SERVING (1 TABLESPOON): ABOUT 25 CALORIES, 0G PROTEIN, 7G CARBOHYDRATE, 0G FAT (0G SATURATED), 0G FIBER, 4G SODIUM

Vanilla-Nectarine
JAM

The beautiful color combination only adds to appeal of this sweet and easy jam.

ACTIVE TIME: 20 MINUTES   **TOTAL TIME:** 35 MINUTES   **MAKES:** 7 (8-OUNCE) JARS

1   vanilla bean

2   pounds nectarines

2   teaspoons lemon zest

2   tablespoons lemon juice

2   cups superfine sugar

1   pound raspberries

3   tablespoons instant pectin (such as Ball RealFruit instant pectin)

1 Scrape out the vanilla seeds into a large bowl. Add the nectarines, and toss with the lemon zest and juice and ¼ cup sugar; let sit for 15 minutes, then toss with the raspberries.

2 In a medium bowl, whisk together 1¾ cups sugar and pectin. Sprinkle the sugar mixture over the fruit, then fold and stir constantly for 3 minutes (do not mash).

3 Transfer to 8-ounce freezer-safe jars (about ¾ cup per jar), leaving a ½ inch of space at the top of each jar.

4 Refrigerate for at least 3 days before serving, or freeze for up to 1 year. If frozen, thaw in the refrigerator overnight before serving (once open, consume within 1 week).

EACH SERVING (1 TABLESPOON): ABOUT 25 CALORIES, 0G PROTEIN, 7G CARBOHYDRATE, 0G FAT (0G SATURATED), 1G FIBER, 4MG SODIUM

TIP

Place a teaspoon of jam on a cold plate and refrigerate for 2 to 3 minutes. If a skin forms and the shape holds when pushed with a finger, the jam has jelled.

Sweet Cherry
JAM

Who can resist homemade cherry jam? Take the time
to find perfectly ripe fruit for the best results.

ACTIVE TIME: 1 HOUR **TOTAL TIME:** 1 HOUR, PLUS PROCESSING **MAKES:** 5 (8-OUNCE) JARS

2	pounds dark sweet cherries
5	cups sugar
¼	cup fresh lemon juice
1	pouch (3 ounces) liquid fruit pectin

1 Prepare 5 (8-ounce) jars and lids (page 9).
Fill the canner halfway with water. Cover; heat
to simmering over High heat.

2 Meanwhile, remove the pits from the cherries;
finely chop enough cherries to equal 3 cups.

3 In a heavy nonreactive 8-quart saucepot,
combine cherries, sugar, and lemon juice; heat to
boiling over High heat, stirring constantly; stir in
pectin. Cook until the mixture comes to a rolling
boil; boil for 1 minute. Remove from the heat.
With a spoon, skim off any foam.

4 Quickly ladle the hot jam into the hot jars to
within ¼ inch of the tops. Wipe the jar rims and
threads clean; cover quickly with the lids, and
screw the bands on securely but not too tightly.
Process in a boiling-water bath (page 8) for
10 minutes; cool jars and test for an airtight seal
(page 10). Makes five (8-ounce) jars.

EACH SERVING (1 TABLESPOON): ABOUT 55 CALORIES,
0G PROTEIN, 14G CARBOHYDRATE, 0G TOTAL FAT
(0G SATURATED), 0G FIBER, 0MG SODIUM.

Tart Cherry Jam

Prepare as directed but substitute **2 pounds tart
cherries** for sweet cherries, use only **4½ cups
sugar,** and omit lemon juice. Remove pits from
cherries and finely chop enough cherries to equal
about 2½ cups. Makes three (8-ounce) jars.

EACH SERVING (1 TABLESPOON): ABOUT 100 CALORIES,
0G PROTEIN, 25G CARBOHYDRATE, 0G TOTAL FAT
(0G SATURATED), 0G FIBER, 1MG SODIUM

Cherry
LINZER BARS

A new take on the traditional Linzer cookie, these fruit-filled bars are a little easier to make but just as delicious.

ACTIVE TIME: 45 MINUTES   **TOTAL TIME:** 1 HOUR AND 20 MINUTES, PLUS COOLING   **MAKES:** ABOUT 36 BARS

½   cup dried tart cherries

1¾ cups all-purpose flour

1   teaspoon ground cinnamon

½   teaspoon baking powder

salt

1   cup hazelnuts (filberts)

½   cup granulated sugar

½   cup packed light brown sugar

¾   cup butter or margarine

½   teaspoon freshly grated lemon peel

1   large egg

1   (8-ounce) jar tart cherry jam

confectioners' sugar (optional)

1 Preheat your oven to 350°F. In a small bowl, combine cherries and 2 tablespoons water; microwave on High for 1 minute. Set aside.

2 Meanwhile, line a 13 x 9-inch baking pan with foil, with foil overhang at the short ends. On waxed paper, combine flour, cinnamon, baking powder, and ¼ teaspoon salt.

3 In a food processor, pulse nuts and sugars until nuts are finely ground. Add butter and lemon peel; pulse until creamy. Blend in egg. Add the flour mixture; pulse just until the mixture comes together.

4 Reserve 1¼ cups dough; chill. With floured fingers, press the remaining dough into the bottom of the prepared pan. Stir the jam into the cherries; spread over the crust, up to ¼ inch from the edges. With your hands, roll the chilled dough into ¼-inch-thick ropes; arrange diagonally, 1½ inches apart, over the jam. Arrange the remaining ropes around the edge of the pan. Bake for 35 minutes or until the dough is golden. Cool in the pan on a wire rack.

5 Transfer to a cutting board. Cut into 36 bars. Store in airtight containers, layered with waxed paper, at room temperature for up to 3 days or in the freezer for up to 1 month. Sprinkle with confectioners' sugar to serve.

EACH SERVING (1 BAR): ABOUT 135 CALORIES, 2G PROTEIN, 19G CARBOHYDRATES, 6G FAT (3G SATURATED), 1G FIBER, 25MG SODIUM

Blueberry
SKILLET JAM

A speedy, no-fuss way to whip up a small batch of super-fruity jam.

ACTIVE TIME: 5 MINUTES **TOTAL TIME:** 15 MINUTES **MAKES:** 2 CUPS

1	pint blueberries
2	tablespoons powdered fruit pectin
½	teaspoon margarine or butter
1	cup sugar

1 In a 12-inch skillet, heat blueberries, pectin, and margarine over Medium-High heat, stirring constantly until the mixture boils. Stir in sugar; heat to boiling. Boil for 1 minute; remove from the heat.

2 Pour the jam into 2 (8-ounce) jars with tight-fitting lids. Cover and refrigerate until the jam is set and cold, about 6 hours. Keep jam refrigerated and use within 3 weeks.

EACH SERVING (1 TABLESPOON): ABOUT 30 CALORIES, 0G PROTEIN, 8G CARBOHYDRATE, 0G TOTAL FAT (0G SATURATED), 0G FIBER, 3MG SODIUM

Raspberry Skillet Jam

Prepare as directed but use **3 cups raspberries**, **1½ cups sugar**, and **1 tablespoon powdered fruit pectin**. (Press half the raspberries through a sieve to remove some seeds before mixing with other ingredients.) Makes about 2 cups.

EACH SERVING (1 TABLESPOON): ABOUT 45 CALORIES, 0G PROTEIN, 11G CARBOHYDRATE, 0G TOTAL FAT (0G SATURATED), 1G FIBER, 2MG SODIUM

Blackberry
PRESERVES

Extend your enjoyment of those juicy, sun-ripened blackberries with a delicious refrigerator preserve.

ACTIVE TIME: 10 MINUTES   **TOTAL TIME:** 30 MINUTES, PLUS COOLING   **MAKES:** 1 (8-OUNCE) JAR

4   cups blackberries

¼   cup fresh lemon juice

4   pieces lemon peel

5   pieces orange peel

1   cup sugar

1 Place blackberries, lemon juice, lemon and orange peels, and ¼ cup water in a medium saucepan, and bring to a boil over Medium-High heat. Reduce heat to Medium-Low and simmer until the berries are soft, 10 to 12 minutes. Remove citrus peels and stir in sugar.

2 Increase the heat to Medium-High, and let the mixture return to a boil. Cook, stirring frequently, until the preserves have jelled, about 7 minutes.

3 Pour into clean glass jars and let cool to room temperature. Store refrigerated for up to 3 weeks.

EACH SERVING (1 TABLESPOON): ABOUT 65 CALORIES, 1G PROTEIN, 16G CARBOHYDRATE, 0G TOTAL FAT (0G SATURATED), 2G FIBER, 1MG SODIUM

TIP

Preserves and jams are very similar, and the terms can be used interchangeably. While both are fruit suspended in a jell, store-bought jams have strict guidelines set by the FDA regarding fruit-to-sugar content. At home, though, the consistency often varies.

Grape Jelly
(page 46)

2 Fruit Butters & Jellies

It is common to confuse jellies and jams, so what's the difference, really? Jellies are the more refined spread. Made from juice, jellies are a strained fruit jell that contains no fruit pulp or other sediments. Jalapeño Pepper Jelly and Champagne & Grape Jelly utilize liquid to make sweet spreads. Similarly, fruit butters are smooth and rich but tend to have deeper flavor than jelly. Enjoy Blushing Apple Butter after harvesting apples in the fall, or pick up a bushel of peaches at the farmers' market to make Peach Butter.

Blushing
APPLE BUTTER

Cranberries added to this recipe tint this apple butter pink.

ACTIVE TIME: 30 MINUTES, PLUS PREPARING JARS AND LIDS   **TOTAL TIME:** 1 HOUR 30 MINUTES
MAKES: 5 (8-OUNCE) JARS

2   lemons

3¾ pounds (8 large) Granny Smith apples, peeled, cored, and thinly sliced

1   cup cranberries

1½ cups apple cider or apple juice

1½ cups sugar

1 From lemons, with vegetable peeler, remove 3 strips (3 x 1 inch each) peel; squeeze 3 tablespoons juice. In a heavy nonreactive 5-quart Dutch oven, combine apples, cranberries, lemon peel and juice, and apple cider; heat to boiling over High heat. Reduce the heat; simmer, stirring occasionally, until apples are very soft, about 10 minutes.

2 Stir in sugar; heat to boiling over High heat. Reduce the heat to Medium; partially cover and cook, stirring occasionally, until apple butter is very thick, about 1 hour. (Mixture may sputter and splash, so be careful when stirring.)

3 Meanwhile, prepare 5 (8-ounce) jars with tight-fitting lids (page 9). Fill the canner halfway with water; cover and heat to simmering over High heat. In batches, puree apple butter until smooth, either in a blender with the center part of the cover removed to let steam escape, or in a food processor with a knife blade attached.

4 Ladle the hot apple butter into clean jars to within ¼ inch of tops. Wipe the jar rims and threads clean. Cover quickly and screw the bands on securely but not too tightly. Process in a boiling-water bath (page 8) for 10 minutes; cool the jars and test for an airtight seal (page 10).

EACH SERVING (1 TABLESPOON): ABOUT 30 CALORIES, 0G PROTEIN, 8G CARBOHYDRATE, 0G TOTAL FAT (0G SATURATED), 0G FIBER, 0MG SODIUM

TIP

Plan ahead: Make a batch to give as gifts during the holidays.

Jalapeño Pepper
JELLY

This is a great accompaniment to meat and chicken dishes. Or dollop it onto crackers spread with cream cheese for a flavor-packed appetizer.

ACTIVE TIME: 20 MINUTES, PLUS PREPARING JARS AND LIDS **TOTAL TIME:** 25 MINUTES, PLUS PROCESSING
MAKES: 6 (8-OUNCE) JARS

8   large green peppers, each cut into quarters

6   jalapeño chilies or hot red chilies, seeded

6   cups sugar

½   cup distilled white vinegar

1   (6-ounce) package liquid fruit pectin

4   drops green food coloring (optional)

1 Prepare 6 (8-ounce) jars and lids (page 9). Fill canner halfway with water. Cover; heat to simmering over High heat.

2 Meanwhile, in a blender or food processor with a knife blade attached, process green peppers and jalapeños until very finely chopped. Transfer the pepper mixture to a sieve set over a large bowl. With a spoon, press the pepper mixture until all liquid is removed. (There should be about 2 cups of liquid.) Discard peppers.

3 In a nonreactive 8-quart saucepot, combine the sugar, pepper liquid, and vinegar; heat to boiling over High heat. Boil for 10 minutes. Stir in pectin and food coloring, if using. Cook, stirring constantly, until the mixture comes to rolling boil; boil for 1 minute. Remove from the heat. With a spoon, skim off any foam.

4 Quickly ladle the hot jelly into hot jars to within ¼ inch of tops. Wipe the jar rims and threads clean; cover quickly with lids and screw bands on securely but not too tightly. Process the jars in a boiling-water bath (page 8) for 10 minutes; cool the jars and test for an airtight seal (page 10).

EACH SERVING (1 TABLESPOON): ABOUT 50 CALORIES, 0G PROTEIN, 13G CARBOHYDRATE, 0G TOTAL FAT (0G SATURATED), 0G FIBER, 0MG SODIUM

ALL-SEASON
Apple Jelly

Try this delicious apple jelly or one of its variations to brighten up your morning toast or glaze a ham or a pork roast.

ACTIVE TIME: 5 MINUTES, PLUS PREPARING JARS AND LIDS **TOTAL TIME:** 15 MINUTES, PLUS PROCESSING
MAKES: 4 (8-OUNCE) JARS

4   cups apple juice
1   (1¾-ounce) package powdered fruit pectin
5   cups sugar

1 Prepare 4 (8-ounce) jars and lids (page 9). Fill a canner halfway with water; cover and heat to simmering over High heat.

2 Meanwhile, in a nonreactive 5-quart Dutch oven, combine apple juice and pectin. Heat to boiling over High heat, stirring constantly; immediately stir in sugar. Cook, stirring constantly, until the mixture comes to a rolling boil; boil for 1 minute. Remove from the heat. With a spoon, skim off any foam.

3 Quickly ladle the hot jelly into hot jars to within ¼ inch of tops. Wipe the jar rims and threads clean; cover quickly with lids and screw the bands on securely but not too tightly. Process in a boiling-water bath (page 8) for 10 minutes; cool the jars and test for an airtight seal (page 10).

EACH SERVING (1 TABLESPOON): ABOUT 70 CALORIES, 0G PROTEIN, 18G CARBOHYDRATE, 0G TOTAL FAT (0G SATURATED), 0G FIBER, 2MG SODIUM

Apple Cider Jelly

Prepare as directed, but substitute **4 cups apple cider** for apple juice.

EACH SERVING (1 TABLESPOON): ABOUT 95 CALORIES, 0G PROTEIN, 24G CARBOHYDRATE, 0G TOTAL FAT (0G SATURATED), 0G FIBER, 4MG SODIUM

Spiced Apple Jelly

With a vegetable peeler, remove peel from **1 large navel orange**. With a string, tie **12 cloves, 2 (3-inch) cinnamon sticks**, and **orange peel** in a double thickness of cheesecloth. Prepare the jelly as directed. Add the spice bag to the pot with the apple juice and pectin. Before ladling the jelly, discard the spice bag.

EACH SERVING (1 TABLESPOON): ABOUT 70 CALORIES, 0G PROTEIN, 18G CARBOHYDRATE, 0G TOTAL FAT (0G SATURATED), 0G FIBER, 2MG SODIUM

Grape
JELLY

This recipe will beat a jar from the supermarket any day and makes a great component of a classic PB&J. For photo, see page 40.

ACTIVE TIME: 5 MINUTES, PLUS PREPARING JARS AND LIDS   **TOTAL TIME:** 15 MINUTES, PLUS PROCESSING
MAKES: 4 (8-OUNCE) JARS

2   cups unsweetened grape juice

1   (1¾-ounce) package powdered fruit pectin

3½ cups sugar

1 Prepare 4 (8-ounce) jars and lids (page 9). Fill the canner halfway with water; cover and heat to simmering over High heat.

2 Meanwhile, in a nonreactive 5-quart Dutch oven, combine grape juice, 1 cup water, and pectin. Heat to boiling over High heat, stirring constantly; immediately stir in sugar. Cook, stirring constantly, until the mixture comes to rolling boil; boil for 1 minute. Remove from the heat. With a spoon, skim off any foam.

3 Quickly ladle the hot jelly into hot jars to within ¼ inch of tops. Wipe the jar rims and threads clean; cover quickly with lids and screw bands on securely but not too tightly. Process in a boiling-water bath (page 8) for 10 minutes; cool the jars and test for an airtight seal (page 10).

EACH SERVING (1 TABLESPOON): ABOUT 65 CALORIES, 0G PROTEIN, 17G CARBOHYDRATE, 0G TOTAL FAT (0G SATURATED), 0G FIBER, 3MG SODIUM

Sugar Syrup & Other Liquids for Canning

Fruit can be canned in syrup, fruit juice, or water. Sugar adds flavor and helps retain the fruit's color, but it is not needed to prevent spoilage. The sweetness of your fruit will determine whether you want a light or heavy syrup.

To make sugar syrup: In a medium nonreactive saucepan, heat water or fruit juice and sugar over High heat, stirring until the sugar has dissolved. If directed, stir in ascorbic acid. Reduce the heat to Low; keep it hot (do not boil) for canning; cool, then chill it for freezing. To keep some fruit from darkening, see page 10.

LIGHT SUGAR SYRUP
4 cups water or juice and **1/3 cup sugar**. Yields 4 1/2 cups.

MEDIUM SUGAR SYRUP
4 cups water or juice and **2 cups sugar**. Yields 5 cups.

HEAVY SUGAR SYRUP
4 cups water or juice and **4 cups sugar**. Yields 6 cups.

HEADSPACE WHEN FREEZING PRODUCE IN SUGAR OR LIQUID

How much headspace you need to leave will depend on the size of the jar and the size of the opening:

Pint jar with wide top: 1/2 inch
Pint jar with narrow top: 3/4 inch
Quart jar with wide top: 1 inch
Quart jar with narrow top: 1 1/2 inch

To make your own fruit juice for preserving, prepare it just before packing the fruit or making the sugar syrup. Place ripe, juicy fruit in a large nonreactive saucepan. With a potato masher or a large spoon, crush the fruit well. Over Low heat, stirring frequently, heat to simmering. Strain the juice through a double layer of cheesecloth; discard the fruit pulp.

Peach
BUTTER

An exquisitely delicious spread that has the rich flavor
of ripe peaches and just a hint of cinnamon.

ACTIVE TIME: 30 MINUTES, PLUS PREPARING JARS AND LIDS
TOTAL TIME: 1 HOUR 30 MINUTES, PLUS PROCESSING   **MAKES:** 4 (8-OUNCE) JARS

6   pounds (18 to 20 medium) ripe peaches,
    peeled, pitted, and cut into quarters

2½ cups sugar

½   teaspoon ground cinnamon

1 In a heavy nonreactive 8-quart saucepot, cook peaches over Medium heat, stirring until very soft, about 20 minutes. Remove from heat. In batches, in a blender with the center part of the cover removed to let steam escape, or in a food processor with knife blade attached, puree peaches until smooth.

2 Return the peach puree to the clean saucepot; stir in sugar and cinnamon. Heat the peach mixture to boiling over High heat. Reduce the heat to Medium-Low; cook, stirring frequently, until the puree has thickened and the mixture mounds when dropped from a spoon, about 1 hour.

3 Meanwhile, prepare 4 (8-ounce) jars and lids (page 9). Fill the canner halfway with water; cover and heat to simmering over High heat.

4 Quickly ladle the simmering peach butter into hot jars to within ¼ inch of tops. (Keep the mixture simmering while filling the jars.) Wipe the jar rims and threads clean; cover quickly with lids and screw bands on securely but not too tightly. Process in a boiling-water bath (page 8) for 10 minutes; cool jars and test for an airtight seal (page 10). Makes four (8-ounce) jars.

EACH SERVING (1 TABLESPOON): ABOUT 45 CALORIES, 0G PROTEIN, 11G CARBOHYDRATE, 0G TOTAL FAT (0G SATURATED), 1G FIBER, 0MG SODIUM

Champagne & Grape
JELLY

This sweet condiment is dressy enough to star on a hors d'oeuvres platter along with sharp cheese, or on crisp crackers.

ACTIVE TIME: 20 MINUTES, PLUS PREPARING JARS AND LIDS **TOTAL TIME:** 20 MINUTES, PLUS PROCESSING
MAKES: 10 (8-OUNCE) JARS

2	cups champagne
2	cups white grape juice
7	cups sugar
1	teaspoon unsalted margarine or butter
2	tablespoons lime juice
1	(3-ounce) package liquid fruit pectin

1 Combine the champagne, grape juice, and sugar in a large saucepan over High heat.

2 Bring to a rolling boil and add margarine, lime juice, and pectin. Boil for exactly 1 minute and remove from heat.

3 Sterilize 10 (8-ounce) jars (page 9). Ladle the hot mixture into the hot jars so that each jar is half full. Cover until set, about 2 to 12 hours.

EACH SERVING (1 TABLESPOON): ABOUT 75 CALORIES, 0G PROTEIN, 19G CARBOHYDRATE, 0G TOTAL FAT (0G SATURATED), 0G FIBER, 1MG SODIUM

Red Currant–Habanero
JELLY

Brush over grilled chicken or pork right before
serving for a spicy punch.

ACTIVE TIME: 15 MINUTES   **TOTAL TIME:** 15 MINUTES, PLUS STRAINING AND PROCESSING
MAKES: 4 (8-OUNCE) JARS

2½ pounds red currants

1   cup spring water

1½ cups sugar

½   teaspoon margarine or butter

¼   cup, plus 2 tablespoons liquid fruit pectin

½   habanero pepper

1 Rinse and drain currants and transfer to a
large saucepan. Using a potato masher, crush
the fruit. Add the spring water, and bring to a
boil over High heat. Boil for 10 minutes. Run
the fruit and any liquid through a sieve or food
mill to remove the seeds. Transfer the puree to a
jelly bag or a colander lined with 4 layers of wet
cheesecloth and let drip overnight.

2 Transfer the juice to a large saucepan,
add sugar, and cook over High heat for about
10 minutes or until sugar dissolves, stirring
occasionally. Bring the mixture to a boil and stir
in margarine. Stir in pectin and cook for exactly
1 minute. Remove from heat and stir in peppers.

3 Immediately ladle the hot jelly into 4 hot,
sterilized 8-ounce canning jars, leaving ¼ inch
of headspace. Securely cap each jar and process
using the boiling-water-canning method for
5 minutes. Store in a cool, dark pantry for up
to 1 year.

EACH SERVING (1 TABLESPOON): ABOUT 30 CALORIES,
0G PROTEIN, 7G CARBOHYDRATE, 0G TOTAL FAT
(0G SATURATED), 0G FIBER, 0MG SODIUM

Pear Marmalade
(page 80)

3 Compotes, Chutneys & Marmalades

Unlike jams and jellies, these spreads do not have pectin, so they cook longer to soften the fruits. Compotes are especially good served over pound cake, or in savory dishes, like Pork Loin with Cherry-Orange Compote. Chutneys offer a nice contrast to hearty dishes, like in our Beef Tenderloin with Citrus-Red Pepper Chutney. Marmalades include pieces of fruit and the peel. The peel's pith contains natural pectin, allowing the slightly bitter spread to thicken. Spread Tangelo Marmalade over a piece of toast or serve Marmalade-Glazed Ham at your next Easter lunch.

BONUS RECIPES

Sour Cream–Vanilla Pound Cake with Rhubarb Compote *(page 58)*, Cottage Cheese Pancakes with Blueberry Compote *(page 60)*, Pork Loin with Cherry-Orange Compote *(page 62)*, Potato Latkes with Apple-Apricot Compote *(page 64)*, Chutney-Glazed Pork Tenderloin *(page 73)*, Beef Tenderloin with Citrus–Red Pepper Chutney *(page 74)*, Marmalade-Glazed Ham *(page 83)*

Spiced Winter Fruit
COMPOTE

A simple dessert that's usually served chilled, fruit compote can trace its history back to colonial times.

ACTIVE TIME: 30 MINUTES **TOTAL TIME:** 40 MINUTES, PLUS STANDING TIME **MAKES:** 18 SERVINGS

2   large navel oranges

½   cup sugar

½   cup brandy

1   cinnamon stick

1   whole star anise

2   large ripe Bartlett pears

1   large Granny Smith apple

1   large Gala or Fuji apple

1   cup dried Calimyrna figs

1   cup dried apricots

1   cup dried plums (prunes)

¼   cup dried sour cherries

1 With a vegetable peeler, from orange(s), remove 3 strips peel (each 3 inches long) and squeeze ¾ cup juice. Set peel and juice aside separately.

2 In a 4-quart saucepan, combine 3½ cups water, sugar, brandy, cinnamon, star anise, and reserved orange peel. Cover and heat to boiling on High; reduce heat to Medium and simmer for 5 minutes.

3 Meanwhile, peel and core pears and apples, then cut each fruit into ¼-inch-thick slices.

4 Stir figs, apricots, plums, and cherries into saucepan; simmer for 5 minutes. Stir in pears and apples and simmer for 10 minutes or until fruit is tender but not mushy, stirring occasionally.

5 Remove the compote from the heat and stir in reserved orange juice. Let stand at least 30 minutes and up to 2 hours. Discard orange peel, cinnamon, and star anise before serving.

EACH SERVING (1 TABLESPOON): ABOUT 125 CALORIES, 1G PROTEIN, 31G CARBOHYDRATE, 0G TOTAL FAT (0G SATURATED), 3G FIBER, 2MG SODIUM

TIP

Spoon the compote over cake, ice cream, or—for a low-fat finale to a meal—top with a dollop of Greek yogurt.

Strawberry-Rhubarb
COMPOTE

Strawberries add sweetness and a blush of pink
to this low-and-slow-cooked compote.

ACTIVE TIME: 10 MINUTES   **TOTAL TIME:** 1 HOUR AND 15 MINUTES   **MAKES:** 1 (5-OUNCE) JAR

2   pounds rhubarb stalks, chopped

1   pound strawberries, chopped

1   cup sugar

¼   cup apple juice

1   tablespoon grated orange zest

½   teaspoon pure vanilla extract

1 In a large heavy-bottomed pot, combine the rhubarb, strawberries, sugar, apple juice, and orange zest. Bring to a simmer over Medium heat.

2 Reduce the heat and gently simmer, stirring occasionally, until the rhubarb has broken down and the mixture has thickened, 55 to 65 minutes; stir in the vanilla.

3 Serve warm, at room temperature or chilled on toast, pancakes, waffles, or ice cream, or with goat or ricotta cheese.

EACH SERVING (1 TABLESPOON): ABOUT 115 CALORIES, 1G PROTEIN, 28G CARBOHYDRATE, 0G TOTAL FAT (0G SATURATED), 3G FIBER, 5MG SODIUM

TIP

Make sure to discard the leaves on the rhubarb—humans cannot digest them.

Sour Cream–Vanilla Pound Cake
WITH RHUBARB COMPOTE

Dense sour cream and vanilla cake is perfect for spring when served with a sweet-and-tart rhubarb compote.

ACTIVE TIME: 25 MINUTES   **TOTAL TIME:** 1 HOUR AND 30 MINUTES   **MAKES:** 8 SERVINGS

POUND CAKE

2½ cups sugar

½   cup unsalted butter or margarine

½   cup sour cream

1   vanilla bean

3   large eggs

1½ cups all-purpose flour

½   teaspoon baking soda

1   teaspoon salt

COMPOTE

1½ pounds rhubarb stalks, chopped

2   teaspoon ground ginger

whipped cream

1 To prepare Pound Cake: Preheat your oven to 375°F. Meanwhile, in the bowl of a stand mixer fitted with a paddle attachment, cream together 1½ cups sugar and butter on medium speed until fluffy, about 4 minutes. Add sour cream and vanilla seeds and mix for 2 minutes. Add eggs, one at a time, fully incorporating each. Add flour, baking soda, and salt, and mix until just combined.

2 Pour the batter into a greased 8 x 4-inch loaf pan and spread evenly with a rubber spatula. Bake until a toothpick inserted into the center comes out clean, 50 minutes to 1 hour. Transfer the pan to a wire rack and let cool for 30 minutes; invert the pan to release the cake and let cool completely on a rack, at least 2 hours.

3 To prepare Compote: In a medium saucepan over Medium-High heat, bring rhubarb, ginger, 2 tablespoons water, and remaining sugar to a boil. Reduce to a simmer and cook until rhubarb is broken down but chunks remain, about 8 to 10 minutes. Remove from heat and let cool completely, at least 2 hours. To serve, cut the cake into 8 slices; top each with a dollop of whipped cream and rhubarb compote.

EACH SERVING: ABOUT 510 CALORIES, 6G PROTEIN, 86G CARBOHYDRATE, 17G TOTAL FAT (10G SATURATED), 2G FIBER, 361MG SODIUM

Cottage Cheese Pancakes
WITH BLUEBERRY COMPOTE

Fresh blueberry compote over fluffy pancakes lends sweetness without additives or empty calories.

ACTIVE TIME: 15 MINUTES   **TOTAL TIME:** 15 MINUTES   **MAKES:** 2 SERVINGS

COMPOTE

1	cup frozen blueberries
1	teaspoon fresh lemon juice
2	tablespoons granulated sugar

PANCAKES

½	cup all-purpose flour
¼	teaspoon baking powder
⅛	teaspoon baking soda
	kosher salt
½	cup low-fat cottage cheese
¼	cup whole milk
2	large egg whites
	canola oil

1 To prepare Compote: In a small saucepan, combine blueberries, lemon juice, and 1 tablespoon of the sugar and bring to a boil. Reduce heat and simmer, stirring occasionally, until slightly thickened and syrupy, 5 to 6 minutes; set aside.

2 To prepare Pancakes: Meanwhile, in a medium bowl, whisk together the flour, baking powder, baking soda, remaining tablespoon sugar, and a pinch of salt.

3 In a second bowl, whisk together the cottage cheese, milk, and egg whites. Add the cottage cheese mixture to the flour mixture and mix until fully incorporated.

4 Heat 1 tablespoon canola oil in a large nonstick skillet over Medium heat. In two batches, drop large spoonfuls (about ¼ cup each) of the batter into the skillet and cook until bubbles begin to appear in the center. Flip the pancakes and cook for 1 minute more; repeat with the remaining batter. Serve with the blueberry compote.

EACH SERVING: ABOUT 295 CALORIES, 14G PROTEIN, 50G CARBOHYDRATE, 5G TOTAL FAT (1G SATURATED), 3G FIBER, 484MG SODIUM

TIP

Use any extra compote on waffles or toast spread with cream cheese.

Pork Loin
WITH CHERRY-ORANGE COMPOTE

This roast is complemented by a zesty and sweet sauce
and would be a show-stopper at any gathering.

ACTIVE TIME: 15 MINUTES **TOTAL TIME:** 1 HOUR AND 45 MINUTES **MAKES:** 12 SERVINGS

PORK LOIN

1½ tablespoons orange zest
   (reserve navel oranges)

2   tablespoons minced garlic

2   tablespoons chopped fresh sage

kosher salt

ground black pepper

1   (4-pound) bone-in pork center loin roast

COMPOTE

2   tablespoons stick margarine or butter

1   cup finely chopped onion

1   cup dry white wine or fresh orange juice

1   cup dried cherries

½   cup golden raisins

2   tablespoons honey

salt

1 To prepare the Pork Loin: Heat oven to 375°F.
2 Mix zest, garlic, sage, 1¼ teaspoons salt,
and ½ teaspoon pepper together in a small bowl.
Rub mixture firmly onto pork.
3 Place pork, bone side down, in a shallow
roasting pan. Roast 1 hour and 15 minutes or
until a meat thermometer inserted into center
of meat, not touching bone, registers 155°F.
Let pork rest for 15 minutes.
1 To prepare the Compote: While the pork
roasts, make the compote: Melt margarine in

a medium saucepan. Add onion; sauté until
translucent. Add wine, cherries, raisins, honey, and
salt to taste. Bring to a boil; reduce heat, cover, and
simmer gently for 15 minutes or until fruits are soft.
Remove the pan from the heat.
5 Cut off the white and any peel remaining on
reserved oranges. Holding oranges over a bowl, cut
between membranes to release sections. Squeeze
juices from membranes into a bowl; cover and reserve.
6 Remove the roast to a serving platter. Add ½ cup
water to the roasting pan. Place the pan over two
burners and stir, scraping up browned bits on the
bottom. Pour into a small bowl or a 1- to 2-cup glass
measure; let stand until the fat rises to the top. Skim
off the fat; reserve the drippings on the bottom.
7 Stir drippings, oranges, and juice into compote.
Heat over Medium-Low heat (don't boil, or orange
sections will break up). Garnish the platter with
herbs and fruit; serve the compote with the pork.

EACH SERVING: ABOUT 320 CALORIES, 25G PROTEIN,
22G CARBOHYDRATE, 15G TOTAL FAT (6G SATURATED),
1G FIBER, 297MG SODIUM

TIP

Pork can be prepared through step 2 up to
2 days ahead. Wrap airtight and refrigerate.
Cut and wrap the onion for the compote and
prepare the orange sections up to 2 days
ahead as well. Cover the container with the
ingredients and keep in the refrigerator.

Potato Latkes
WITH APPLE-APRICOT COMPOTE

Potato pancakes can be made to shine and are easily the centerpiece of a comforting and casual autumn meal.

ACTIVE TIME: 35 MINUTES   **TOTAL TIME:** 1 HOUR AND 5 MINUTES   **MAKES:** 6 SERVINGS

LATKES

3	Yukon gold potatoes, grated
1	medium onion, chopped
1	large egg
3	tablespoons matzo meal

salt

ground black pepper

vegetable oil

COMPOTE

3	firm, sweet apples (such as Gala or Fuji)
¼	cup light brown sugar
2	tablespoons lemon juice
1	teaspoon grated fresh ginger
¼	teaspoon dried mustard
⅓	cup dried apricots
¼	cup golden raisins

1 To prepare the Latkes: Place small batches of grated potatoes in the center of a dish towel, gather up the sides of the towel, and wring excess liquid from the potatoes. Transfer potatoes to a large bowl and repeat with the remaining potatoes. Add onion, egg, matzo meal, 1 teaspoon salt, and ½ teaspoon pepper to the potatoes, mix well, and set aside.

2 Heat ¼ inch of oil in a 12-inch skillet over Medium heat. Add the potato mixture by the ¼-cupful to the hot oil, lightly flatten pancakes with a spatula, and cook latkes until golden, about 5 minutes. Turn over and cook until heated through and golden brown, about 5 more minutes. Serve warm.

3 To prepare the Compote: Combine apples, brown sugar, lemon juice, ginger, and mustard in a small saucepan over Medium-Low heat and cook, stirring occasionally, for 10 minutes.

4 Add apricots, raisins, and ¼ cup water, cover, and cook for 10 more minutes.

5 Lightly mash the compote with the back of a wooden spoon, cover, and cook for 5 more minutes. Transfer to a bowl and set aside.

EACH SERVING (2 LATKES WITH 1 TABLESPOON COMPOTE): ABOUT 250 CALORIES, 4G PROTEIN, 54G CARBOHYDRATE, 3G TOTAL FAT (0G SATURATED), 5G FIBER, 376MG SODIUM

TIP

To ensure the crispiest of latkes, be sure to thoroughly wring as much moisture as you can from the grated potatoes.

Apple-Fig
COMPOTE

Try this compote warm or chilled, spooned over ice cream or pound cake for dessert or topped with plain yogurt for breakfast.

ACTIVE TIME: 5 MINUTES   **TOTAL TIME:** 25 MINUTES   **MAKES:** 6 CUPS

1   lemon

2   pounds Rome Beauty or Jonagold apples, peeled, cored, and chopped

1½   cups apple cider

1   (6-ounce) package dried Calimyrna figs

½   cup dried tart cherries

⅓   cup sugar

1   stick cinnamon

1 From lemon, remove peel with vegetable peeler in 1-inch-wide strips, then squeeze 2 tablespoons juice.

2 In a 4-quart saucepan, combine lemon peel and juice, apples, cider, figs, cherries, sugar, and cinnamon; cover and heat to boiling over High heat. Reduce the heat to Medium-Low; simmer, covered, 20 minutes or until apples are tender, stirring occasionally.

3 Pour the fruit mixture into a bowl; serve warm, or cover and refrigerate to serve within 4 days.

EACH SERVING (1 TABLESPOON): ABOUT 15 CALORIES, 0G PROTEIN, 4G CARBOHYDRATE, 0G TOTAL FAT (0G SATURATED), 0G FIBER, 0MG SODIUM

Fig
CHUTNEY

Calimyrna figs have light-colored flesh and skin. If you cannot find them, black Mission figs also work well.

ACTIVE TIME: 30 MINUTES   **TOTAL TIME:** 40 MINUTES   **MAKES:** 4 CUPS

olive oil

1   medium onion, chopped

2   Granny Smith apples

12 ounces dried Calimyrna figs (2 cups)

½   cup dry red wine

½   cup sugar

1   teaspoon grated fresh lemon peel, plus additional for garnish

salt

1 In a 4-quart saucepan, heat 1 tablespoon oil on Medium until hot. Add chopped onion; cook for 10 to 12 minutes or until golden, stirring occasionally.

2 To the onion in the saucepan, add apples, figs, 1 cup water, wine, sugar, grated lemon peel, and ¼ teaspoon salt; heat to boiling on High, stirring occasionally. Reduce heat to Medium; cover and cook for 10 minutes. Uncover and cook for 10 minutes longer or until the figs are tender and the mixture thickens, stirring frequently to prevent scorching.

3 Serve the chutney warm or at room temperature. Garnish with the lemon peel.

EACH SERVING (¼ CUP): ABOUT 110 CALORIES, 1G PROTEIN, 24G CARBOHYDRATE, 1G TOTAL FAT (0G SATURATED), 3G FIBER, 32MG SODIUM

TIP

The chutney can be prepared completely up to a week ahead. In fact, this allows the flavors to blend even more. Make sure to let it stand for about an hour at room temperature before serving—or reheat it if you prefer it warm.

Home-Style
CHUTNEY

This chutney gets its full flavor from a tempting mix of fruits; it is a fine accompaniment to grilled lamb or a cheese plate.

ACTIVE TIME: 40 MINUTES **TOTAL TIME:** 2 HOURS AND 15 MINUTES, PLUS PROCESSING **MAKES:** 6 (8-OUNCE) JARS

2–3 medium oranges

3 pounds (6 large) ripe nectarines, pitted and cut into wedges

1½ pounds (3 large) Granny Smith apples, peeled, cored, and cut into half-inch pieces

1 pound (3 medium) firm-ripe tomatoes, cut into half-inch pieces

3 medium onions, cut into half-inch pieces

3 tablespoons minced, peeled fresh ginger

1 (16-ounce) package light brown sugar

2¼ cups distilled white vinegar

2 teaspoons dry mustard

salt

¼ teaspoon cayenne pepper

1 cup dark seedless raisins

1 From oranges, grate 2 tablespoons peel and squeeze ⅔ cup juice. In a nonreactive 5-quart Dutch oven, combine nectarines, apples, tomatoes, onions, ginger, orange peel and juice, brown sugar, vinegar, mustard, 1 teaspoon salt, and cayenne. Heat to boiling over High heat, stirring frequently. Reduce the heat and simmer for 1 hour. Add raisins; cook, stirring frequently, until the mixture is very thick, about 45 minutes.

2 Meanwhile, prepare 6 (8-ounce) jars and lids (page 9). Fill the canner halfway with water; cover and heat to simmering over High heat.

3 Ladle the simmering chutney into hot jars to within ¼ inch of tops. (Keep the chutney simmering while filling jars.) Wipe the jar rims and threads clean; cover quickly with lids and screw bands on securely but not too tightly. Process in a boiling-water bath (page 8) for 10 minutes; cool the jars and test for an airtight seal (page 10).

EACH SERVING (1 TABLESPOON): ABOUT 35 CALORIES, 0G PROTEIN, 9G CARBOHYDRATE, 0G TOTAL FAT (0G SATURATED), 1G FIBER, 27MG SODIUM

Cranberry-Apple
CHUTNEY

Spiced and sweet, this cranberry-sauce alternative bursts with the bright flavors of fresh fruit.

ACTIVE TIME: 20 MINUTES   **TOTAL TIME:** 55 MINUTES   **MAKES:** 4 CUPS

canola oil

1   large onion

1   tablespoon grated fresh ginger

1   teaspoon ground allspice

2   sticks cinnamon

1   cup sugar

4   cups cranberries

1   cup dried apricots

1   cup apricot nectar

1   teaspoon grated lemon zest

2   tablespoons lemon juice

kosher salt

ground black pepper

2   large Golden Delicious apples, peeled, cored, and chopped into ½-inch chunks

1 Heat 1 tablespoon oil in a large saucepan over Medium-Low heat; add onion, ginger, allspice, and cinnamon sticks. Cook, stirring the mixture frequently, until onion is translucent and tender, for about 10 minutes.

2 Stir in sugar, cranberries, apricots, nectar, lemon zest and juice, 1 teaspoon salt, and ½ teaspoon pepper. Stir the mixture to dissolve sugar, then bring to a boil over High heat; reduce the heat to Medium-Low and simmer for 22 minutes. Stir in apples. Continue to simmer for 10 to 12 minutes longer, stirring once or twice, or until apples are tender yet still hold their shape.

3 Remove from the heat and transfer to a serving bowl. Cover the surface with plastic wrap. Cool at room temperature for 30 minutes, then refrigerate for several hours until chutney is well chilled and has set up.

EACH SERVING (1 TABLESPOON): ABOUT 30 CALORIES, 0G PROTEIN, 7G CARBOHYDRATE, 0G TOTAL FAT (0G SATURATED), 1G FIBER, 31MG SODIUM

TIP

This chutney can be made up to 3 days before serving and stored for up to 4 days.

Quince
CHUTNEY

Try making a batch of this flavorful condiment, packaging it decoratively, and offering it as a gift to your hosts.

ACTIVE TIME: 25 MINUTES   **TOTAL TIME:** 1 HOUR AND 20 MINUTES   **MAKES:** 4 CUPS

1   **(8-ounce) package fresh or frozen cranberries, thawed**

1   **cup onion**

¾   **cup light brown sugar**

1   **cup orange juice**

¼   **cup apple cider vinegar**

1   **tablespoon garlic**

4   **quinces**

½   **cup dried currants**

2   **tablespoons chopped crystallized ginger**

¼   **cup honey**

1   **teaspoon grated lemon rind**

1 In a 4-quart saucepan, combine cranberries, onion, brown sugar, ½ cup orange juice, vinegar, and garlic. Bring to a boil over High heat and cover. Reduce heat to Low and simmer 15 minutes, stirring occasionally.

2 Stir in quinces, currants, remaining ½ cup orange juice, and ginger. Cover and cook until quinces are fork-tender, 30 to 40 minutes. Remove from heat and stir in honey and lemon rind. Let cool for 15 minutes. Transfer to an airtight container and store, refrigerated, for up to 1 week.

EACH SERVING (1 TABLESPOON): ABOUT 30 CALORIES, 0G PROTEIN, 7G CARBOHYDRATE, 0G TOTAL FAT (0G SATURATED), 0G FIBER, 2MG SODIUM

Tomato
CHUTNEY

Serve this tangy-sweet condiment hot or cold
with grilled meats or spread on bread.

ACTIVE TIME: 50 MINUTES   **TOTAL TIME:** 1 HOUR AND 30 MINUTES   **MAKES:** 3¹/2 CUPS

3   pounds ripe tomatoes

2   garlic cloves

1   medium Granny Smith apple

1   small onion

½   cup cider vinegar

⅓   cup packed brown sugar

⅓   cup golden raisins

2   tablespoons gingerroot, peeled and minced

salt

ground black pepper

1 In a 12-inch skillet, heat all ingredients, plus ½ teaspoon salt and ½ teaspoon pepper, to boiling over High heat. Reduce the heat to Medium; cook, uncovered, for 45 to 50 minutes, stirring occasionally, until the mixture thickens.
2 Spoon the chutney into a bowl; cover and refrigerate until well chilled. Use within 2 weeks.

EACH SERVING (1 TABLESPOON): ABOUT 60 CALORIES, 1G PROTEIN, 15G CARBOHYDRATE, 0G TOTAL FAT (0G SATURATED), 1G FIBER, 0MG SODIUM

Spicy Rhubarb
CHUTNEY

This chutney is used to glaze our Chutney-Glazed Pork Tenderloin (page 73) and also makes an excellent condiment for baked ham or lamb chops.

ACTIVE TIME: 10 MINUTES   **TOTAL TIME:** 35 MINUTES   **MAKES:** 2 CUPS

1¼ pounds rhubarb stalks

½ cup light brown sugar

¼ cup apple cider vinegar

¼ cup chopped onion

½ teaspoon ground coriander

½ teaspoon ground ginger

¼ teaspoon dry mustard

salt

⅓ cup dried apricots

⅓ cup dried cherries

2 tablespoons chopped fresh cilantro leaves

1 Wash rhubarb, chop coarsely, and set aside.

2 In a 4-quart saucepan, combine brown sugar, vinegar, onion, coriander, ginger, mustard, and ¼ teaspoon salt. Bring to a boil. Cook over High heat, uncovered, for 3 minutes, stirring constantly.

3 Stir in rhubarb, apricots, and cherries; reduce the heat to Medium-Low and let simmer until rhubarb is just tender but not broken up, 10 to 15 minutes. Remove from heat, stir in cilantro, and let cool for 10 minutes. Refrigerate until ready to use.

EACH SERVING (1 TABLESPOON): ABOUT 25 CALORIES, 0G PROTEIN, 6G CARBOHYDRATE, 0G FAT (0G SATURATED), 1G FIBER, 20MG SODIUM

Chutney-Glazed
PORK TENDERLOIN

A smart choice for a weeknight meal, this dish can
be on the table in less than an hour.

ACTIVE TIME: 10 MINUTES   **TOTAL TIME:** 55 MINUTES   **MAKES:** 4 SERVINGS

vegetable oil cooking spray

1   teaspoon hot paprika

salt

ground black pepper

1   boneless pork tenderloin

1   cup Spicy Rhubarb Chutney
    (prepared or page 72)

tortillas and fresh cilantro sprigs, for serving

1 Preheat your oven to 350°F. Lightly coat the bottom of a roasting pan with cooking spray. In a small bowl, combine paprika, ½ teaspoon salt, and ¼ teaspoon pepper. Sprinkle the mixture over the pork.

2 Place the pork in the prepared roasting pan and roast for 20 minutes. Brush ½ cup Spicy Rhubarb Chutney over tenderloin and continue roasting, 20 to 25 minutes longer, until the internal temperature reaches 160°F, basting occasionally with the pan drippings. Let rest for 10 minutes before slicing.

3 Serve pork tenderloin with the remaining chutney, tortillas, and cilantro, if desired.

EACH SERVING: ABOUT 270 CALORIES, 30G PROTEIN, 25G CARBOHYDRATE, 5G FAT (2G SATURATED), 2G FIBER, 435MG SODIUM

Beef Tenderloin with
CITRUS–RED PEPPER CHUTNEY

Tired of turkey and ham at Christmas dinner? Try this flavorful beef tenderloin with delicious red pepper chutney.

ACTIVE TIME: 20 MINUTES   **TOTAL TIME:** 1 HOUR AND 15 MINUTES   **MAKES:** 12 SERVINGS

BEEF

vegetable oil

ground black pepper

½   teaspoon ground coriander

3   teaspoons mustard seeds

1   beef tenderloin

kosher salt

CHUTNEY

½   cup orange marmalade

¼   cup white wine vinegar

3   tablespoons sugar

1   teaspoon fennel seeds

2   oranges

1½   cups chopped roasted red peppers

bay leaves and pink peppercorns, for garnish

1 To prepare the Beef: Preheat your oven to 450°F. Line a roasting pan or jelly-roll pan with foil. Add a roasting rack to the pan.

2 In a medium bowl, stir together 1 tablespoon oil, 2 teaspoons pepper, coriander, and 2 teaspoons mustard seeds; rub all over the tenderloin. Sprinkle the beef with 1 tablespoon salt. Place the beef on the rack and roast for 40 to 50 minutes or until desired doneness (140°F for medium-rare). Cover loosely with foil and let rest for at least 10 minutes.

3 To prepare the Chutney: Meanwhile, in a 2-quart saucepan, heat marmalade, vinegar, sugar, fennel seeds, and remaining 1 teaspoon mustard seeds on Medium-Low just until marmalade melts, stirring to combine. Remove from the heat; let cool.

4 While the chutney cools, from oranges, cut and discard peel and pith; cut out segments between membranes. Stir orange segments and red peppers into chutney. Place the beef on a platter; garnish with bay leaves and pink peppercorns. Serve with chutney.

EACH SERVING: ABOUT 435 CALORIES, 27G PROTEIN, 17G CARBOHYDRATE, 28G FAT (11G SATURATED), 2G FIBER, 612MG SODIUM

Orange-Cardamom
MARMALADE

This preserved Orange-Cardamom Marmalade makes a tasty gift.
Be sure to add a "made on" date to the label.

ACTIVE TIME: 20 MINUTES   **TOTAL TIME:** 1 HOUR AND 20 MINUTES   **MAKES:** 11 (8-OUNCE) JARS

2½ pounds oranges (such as Valencia or Cara cara)

¾   pound lemons

20   green cardamom pods, crushed

8   cups granulated sugar

1 Prepare the fruit 12 to 24 hours before you plan to cook and preserve the marmalade. Wash and pat dry all the fruit. Trim and discard the stem ends. Cut the oranges and lemons into quarters and poke out all the seeds with the tip of a paring knife. Reserve the seeds in a small covered container. Using a sharp chef's knife or a mandoline slicer, cut all the citrus, including the rinds, into-inch-thick slices.

2 Put the sliced fruit in a large pot, including any juices left on the cutting board. Add 6 cups cold water. Gently press down on the fruit to make sure it is submerged. Cover the pot and set aside at room temperature for 12 to 24 hours. (This softens the rinds and releases the pectin.)

3 The next day, bring the pot of sliced fruit and water to a boil over Medium-High heat. Adjust the heat so the mixture boils steadily without splattering, and cook for 30 minutes. Wrap the crushed cardamom pods and the reserved lemon and orange seeds in a cheesecloth bag tied securely with kitchen twine.

4 While the fruit is cooking, prepare the preserving jars and bring water to a boil in a boiling-water bath. Sterilize the jars and lids.

5 Add the sugar to the fruit mixture and stir until dissolved. Add the cheesecloth bag of cardamom and seeds. Continue to cook the marmalade at a steady boil until it reaches the jell stage (see tip on page 79), or reaches 220°F on a candy thermometer, 30 to 40 minutes longer.

6 Remove the cheesecloth bag from the marmalade, pressing any liquids back into the pan.

7 Remove the marmalade from the heat.

8 Using a wide-mouthed funnel and filling one jar at a time, ladle the marmalade into hot, sterilized jars, leaving ½ inch of headspace. Remove any air bubbles by running a long wooden utensil, such as a chopstick or a wooden skewer, between the jar and the marmalade. Wipe the rims clean and seal. Process the jars in a boiling-water bath (page 8) for 10 minutes and then turn off the heat. Wait 5 minutes and then lift the canning rack and, using a canning jar lifter, transfer the jars to a towel-lined, sturdy, rimmed baking sheet and let them rest. Check the seals, wipe the jars, and label. Store the jars in a cool, dark place for up to 1 year.

EACH SERVING (1 TABLESPOON): ABOUT 40 CALORIES, 0G PROTEIN, 10G CARBOHYDRATE, 0G FAT (0G SATURATED), 0G FIBER, 0G SODIUM

Tangelo
MARMALADE

Making a marmalade from tangelos gives this fruity
spread an intensely complex citrus flavor.

ACTIVE TIME: 30 MINUTES   **TOTAL TIME:** 1 HOUR AND 30 MINUTES   **MAKES:** 3½ CUPS

3   pounds tangelos

1   vanilla bean

4   cups sugar

½   Granny Smith apple

1 Wash and quarter the tangelos. Over a medium
bowl and using a handheld juicer, juice the fruit.
2 Peel the rinds from the juiced segments. Slice
the rinds into ¼-inch-wide strips and discard the
rest of the fruit. Over a small bowl, split vanilla
bean and scrape seeds (reserving both the pod
and the seeds).

3 In a large Dutch oven, combine juice, rinds,
and vanilla pod and seeds with sugar, 1 cup water,
and apple. Bring to a boil, then reduce heat to
Low and simmer, stirring occasionally, until rinds
are tender and liquid is thickened, about 1 hour.
Remove and discard apple and vanilla-bean pod.
4 Set marmalade aside to cool completely, about
1 hour. Transfer to a large, clean glass jar and
store, refrigerated, for up to 2 weeks.

EACH SERVING (1 TABLESPOON): ABOUT 70 CALORIES,
0G PROTEIN, 18G CARBOHYDRATE, 0G FAT (0G
SATURATED), 1G FIBER, 0G SODIUM

TIP

Here's an easy way to check whether the
marmalade is set: Put a small plate in
the freezer. When the marmalade looks thick
and a bit jelled, put a small amount of the
marmalade on the frozen plate and return
it to the freezer. After a couple of minutes,
run your finger or a spoon down the center
of the marmalade and see if it stays separated
and is a bit wrinkled. If so, it is done.

Pear
MARMALADE

Pears are combined with thinly sliced orange peel, fresh ginger, and a touch of allspice to make an unusually delectable spread.

ACTIVE TIME: 30 MINUTES, PLUS PREPARING JARS AND LIDS   **TOTAL TIME:** 1 HOUR, PLUS PROCESSING
MAKES: 7 (8-OUNCE) JARS

3   large oranges

6   pounds (12 large) pears, peeled, cored, and coarsely chopped (12 cups)

2   tablespoons fresh ginger, peeled and minced

4   cups sugar

⅓   cup fresh lemon juice

½   teaspoon ground allspice

1 From oranges, with a vegetable peeler, remove peel along with some white pith. Cut enough peel into 2 x ⅛-inch strips to equal ¾ cup. Coarsely chop enough oranges to equal 1½ cups; discard seeds.

2 In a heavy nonreactive 8-quart saucepot, combine pears, oranges and orange peel, ginger, sugar, lemon juice, and allspice; heat to boiling over High heat, stirring frequently. Reduce the heat to Medium-High; cook, stirrin to simmering over High heat.

3 Meanwhile, prepare 7 (8-ounce) jars and lids (page 9). Fill a canner halfway with water; cover and heat to simmering over High heat.

4 Quickly ladle the simmering marmalade into hot jars to within ¼ inch of tops. (Keep marmalade simmering while filling the jars.) Wipe the jar rims and threads clean; cover quickly with lids and screw bands on securely but not too tightly. Process in a boiling-water bath (page 8) for 15 minutes; cool the jars and test for an airtight seal (page 10).

EACH SERVING (1 TABLESPOON): ABOUT 40 CALORIES, 0G PROTEIN, 11G CARBOHYDRATE, 0G FAT (0G SATURATED), 0MG SODIUM

TIP

Use any variety of pear you like; this recipe will work with whatever is in season or being sold at your supermarket.

Red Onion–Cherry
MARMALADE

Pungent red onion is cooked with sweet-tart cherries
and other ingredients to create a unique sweet-and-savory condiment.

ACTIVE TIME: 10 MINUTES **TOTAL TIME:** 50 MINUTES **MAKES:** 4½ CUPS

3   large red onions

1   pound pitted tart cherries

2   cups dry red wine (such as Chianti)

1½ cups sugar

2   sticks cinnamon

3   strips lemon zest

salt

1 In a large pot over Medium-High heat, bring all ingredients plus ¼ teaspoon salt to a boil. Reduce the heat to Medium-Low and simmer, stirring once or twice, until onions are deep red and cherries burst, 30 to 40 minutes. Set aside to cool.

2 Transfer to a large glass jar and store, refrigerated, for up to 2 weeks. Serve with roast pork or poultry, or pair with goat cheese and crackers.

EACH SERVING (1 TABLESPOON): ABOUT 25 CALORIES, 0G PROTEIN, 6G CARBOHYDRATE, 0G FAT (0G SATURATED), 0G FIBER, 9MG SODIUM

Marmalade-Glazed
HAM

A sweet and spicy glaze creates a wonderful
caramelized crust on this tender ham.

ACTIVE TIME: 10 MINUTES   **TOTAL TIME:** 1 HOUR AND 15 MINUTES   **MAKES:** 20 SERVINGS

¾   cup Orange-Cardamom Marmalade
     (prepared or page 77)

2   tablespoons dark brown sugar

2   tablespoons red wine vinegar

2   tablespoons grainy Dijon mustard

2   garlic cloves

1   tablespoon fresh rosemary leaves

1   fully cooked, spiral-sliced, smoked, bone-in,
     reduced-sodium half ham

fresh herbs, small apples, and pears,
     for garnish

1 Preheat your oven to 375°F. In a medium
bowl, stir together marmalade, sugar, vinegar,
mustard, garlic, and rosemary. Place the ham in
a 13 x 9-inch roasting pan. Spread the marmalade
mixture on the skin sides of the ham.

2 Bake the ham for 1 hour to 1 hour and
15 minutes, or until a golden-brown crust forms
and a meat thermometer inserted horizontally
in the bottom portion of the ham (not touching
the bone) reaches 140°F.

3 Transfer the ham to a serving platter and
garnish with herbs and fruit before serving.

EACH SERVING: ABOUT 220 CALORIES, 19G PROTEIN,
8G CARBOHYDRATE, 14G FAT (4G SATURATED),
0G FIBER, 1,103MG SODIUM

Classic Dill Pickles
(page 91)

4 Pickles & Relishes

Cool, crunchy and delightfully tangy, a good pickle can be a tasty snack or the perfect addition to your sandwich. Whether you prefer Quick Sweet Pickles or Classic Dill Pickles, there is no doubt that pickles can be incorporated into any meal. And did you know that they were easy to make at home, too? A homemade batch can be made in under an hour! And don't stop there—relishes like Quick Sauerkraut and Corn Relish utilize the same vinegar-based liquids to preserve fresh flavors. Once you've mastered pickling cucumbers, the rest is no big dill.

BONUS RECIPES

Cheeseburger Tostada with Homemade Pickles (*page 93*), **Pork & Sauerkraut Stir-Fry** (*page 96*), **Reuben Macaroni and Cheese** (*page 97*)

QUICK
Sweet Pickles

Persian isn't your usual pickling cucumber, but it's perfect
for this eat-right-away snack.

ACTIVE TIME: 15 MINUTES   **TOTAL TIME:** 15 MINUTES PLUS PROCESSING   **MAKES:** 8 SERVINGS

⅔   cup white-wine vinegar or apple
     cider vinegar

⅓   cup sugar

salt

2   cups thinly sliced Persian cucumbers
     (about 2 cucumbers)

2   red onions

2   tablespoons torn dill sprigs

1   teaspoon whole peppercorns

olive oil

1 In a medium bowl, mix vinegar, sugar, and
⅛ teaspoon salt, stirring occasionally, until sugar
dissolves. Set aside.

2 In a nonreactive bowl, combine cucumbers,
onions, dill, and peppercorns. Add 3 tablespoons
olive oil to the reserved vinegar mixture and stir
well. Pour over vegetables and toss to combine.
Cover the bowl and refrigerate for at least 8 hours
before serving. Store pickles, refrigerated, for up
to 5 days.

EACH SERVING: ABOUT 30 CALORIES, 1G PROTEIN,
5G CARBOHYDRATE, 1G FAT (0G SATURATED), 1G FIBER,
16MG SODIUM

Bread & Butter
PICKLES

Take a jar of these sweet pickles to your next family barbecue, or just use them to perk up a tuna sandwich.

ACTIVE TIME: 20 MINUTES, PLUS PREPARING JARS AND LIDS **TOTAL TIME:** 45 MINUTES, PLUS PROCESSING
MAKES: 6 (16-OUNCE) JARS

4   pounds kirby cucumbers (4 to 6 inches long), cut into ¼-inch-thick slices

3   large onions, thinly sliced

½   cup kosher, canning, or pickling salt

8   cups ice cubes (3 trays)

5   cups sugar

5   cups cider vinegar

1   teaspoon ground turmeric

1½   teaspoons celery seeds

1½   teaspoons mustard seeds

1 In an 8-quart enamel, stainless steel, or glass container, combine cucumbers, onions, salt, and enough cold water to cover. Stir until salt has dissolved; stir in ice. Cover and let stand in a cool place for 3 hours. Drain the vegetables and rinse with cold running water; drain.

2 In a nonreactive 8-quart saucepot, combine sugar, vinegar, turmeric, celery seeds, and mustard seeds; heat to boiling over High heat. Reduce the heat; simmer, stirring for 30 minutes.

3 Meanwhile, prepare 6 (16-ounce) jars and lids (page 9). Fill a canner halfway with water; cover and heat to simmering over High heat.

4 Add cucumbers and onions to pot; heat to boiling. Spoon the hot vegetables into hot jars to within ½ inch of tops. Immediately ladle the simmering syrup over the vegetables to within ¼ inch of tops, making sure the vegetables are completely covered in the syrup. (Keep the syrup simmering while filling the jars.) Wipe the jar rims and threads clean; cover quickly with lids and screw bands on securely but not too tightly. Process in a boiling-water bath (page 8) for 10 minutes; cool the jars and test for an airtight seal (page 10).

EACH SERVING (¼ CUP): ABOUT 95 CALORIES, 0G PROTEIN, 25G CARBOHYDRATE, 0G FAT (0G SATURATED), 0G FIBER, 292MG SODIUM

Cornichon-Style
PICKLES

Cornichons—French for *gherkins*—are tart pickles made from tiny cucumbers, which can be hard to find. Our alternative is delicious.

ACTIVE TIME: 30 MINUTES   **TOTAL TIME:** 2½ HOURS, PLUS PROCESSING   **MAKES:** 2 (16-OUNCE) JARS

2   pounds small pickling cucumbers

½   cup kosher salt

2   cups white distilled vinegar (5% acidity)

1   garlic clove

1   tablespoon chopped onion

½   tablespoon peppercorns

2   whole cloves

2   bay leaves

1 Prepare the cucumbers: In a large, nonreactive bowl, toss cucumbers with ¼ cup plus 2 tablespoons salt. Transfer to a cheesecloth-lined colander and let drain for 2 hours. Rinse cucumbers thoroughly with cold water and set aside.

2 Combine vinegar, 2 cups water, and remaining salt in a small saucepan over High heat and bring to a boil; reduce the heat to Medium and set aside.

3 Sterilize 2 (16-ounce) jars and keep hot. Divide the garlic, onion, peppercorns, cloves, and bay leaves between the jars. Add the cucumbers up to ½ inch from the top of each jar.

4 Pour the hot vinegar mixture over the cucumbers, leaving ¼ inch of headspace. Remove any air bubbles, securely cap each jar, and process using the boiling-water canning method (page 9) for 10 minutes.

5 Cool jars, check for proper seals, and store in a cool, dark place at least 3 weeks before opening.

EACH SERVING: ABOUT 10 CALORIES, 0G PROTEIN, 2G CARBOHYDRATE, 0G FAT (0G SATURATED), 1G FIBER, 482MG SODIUM

TIP
These pickles will keep for up to 1 year. Thoroughly cooled, unprocessed pickles will keep refrigerated for up to 1 month.

CLASSIC
Dill Pickles

These are a staple to have in your fridge and are best alongside your favorite sandwich.

ACTIVE TIME: 10 MINUTES **TOTAL TIME:** 10 MINUTES, PLUS PROCESSING **MAKES:** 1 (32-OUNCE) JAR

1¼ cups distilled white vinegar

4 garlic cloves, crushed and peeled

3 tablespoons sugar

kosher salt

1 pound kirby or pickling cucumbers, quartered lengthwise

3 sprigs dill

1 In a small pot, combine white vinegar, 1 cup water, garlic, sugar, and 2 tablespoons salt. Heat on Medium until sugar dissolves, stirring.

2 Arrange cucumber spears and dill in a 32-ounce jar; pour warm brine over cucumbers to cover. (Can be made in 2 or more smaller jars as long as there's enough brine to cover.) Let cool slightly.

3 Screw on the lid and refrigerate for at least 4 hours or up to 2 weeks.

EACH SERVING: ABOUT 10 CALORIES, 0G PROTEIN, 2G CARBOHYDRATE, 0G FAT (0G SATURATED), 0G FIBER, 240MG SODIUM

Cheeseburger Tostada
WITH HOMEMADE PICKLES

This is an easy American twist on classic Mexican fare.
Use homemade pickles to add some zing.

ACTIVE TIME: 10 MINUTES   **TOTAL TIME:** 22 MINUTES   **MAKES:** 4 SERVINGS

4   medium flour tortillas

nonstick cooking spray

1   (8-ounce) package ground beef

1   cup shredded Cheddar cheese

salt

shredded lettuce, chopped tomatoes,
  Classic Dill Pickles, chopped
  (prepared or page 91), ketchup,
  for serving

1 Arrange tortillas on 2 cookie sheets sprayed with nonstick cooking spray. Top with beef, cheese, and ¼ teaspoon salt. Bake at 475°F for 12 minutes.

2 Top with lettuce, tomatoes, and Classic Dill Pickles. Drizzle with ketchup, if desired.

EACH SERVING: ABOUT 385 CALORIES, 23G PROTEIN, 30G CARBOHYDRATE, 19G FAT (9G SATURATED), 2G FIBER, 1,028MG SODIUM

Watermelon Rind
PICKLES

This "pickled" topping uses the white part of a watermelon rind
to create a sweet and savory condiment.

ACTIVE TIME: 15 MINUTES   **TOTAL TIME:** 30 MINUTES   **MAKES:** 1½ CUPS

1	baby watermelon
½	cup cider vinegar
⅓	cup sugar
1	cinnamon stick
¼	teaspoon fennel seeds

salt

1 With a vegetable peeler, remove the green peel of the watermelon. Cut off the white rind; reserve the watermelon for another use.

2 Cut the rind into ¼-inch cubes until you have 2 cups.

3 In 12-inch skillet, combine rind, cider vinegar, sugar, cinnamon stick, fennel seeds, and ½ teaspoon salt. Simmer on Medium for 15 minutes, stirring occasionally.

4 Cool the pickles; serve with grilled pork or chicken.

EACH SERVING (¼ CUP): ABOUT 85 CALORIES, 0G
PROTEIN, 22G CARBOHYDRATE, 0G FAT
(0G SATURATED), 0G FIBER, 177MG SODIUM

Corn
RELISH

Jars of colorful corn relish are pretty enough to share with friends.

ACTIVE TIME: 40 MINUTES, PLUS PREPARING JARS AND LIDS   **TOTAL TIME:** 1 HOUR 15 MINUTES, PLUS PROCESSING   **MAKES:** 5 (16-OUNCE) JARS

12   ears corn, husks and silk removed

2   green peppers, finely chopped (1½ cups)

2   red peppers, finely chopped (1½ cups)

1   pound firm-ripe medium tomatoes, chopped (1½ cups)

2   medium onions, chopped (1 cup)

1½   cups sugar

3   cups cider vinegar

kosher, canning, or pickling salt

1   teaspoon celery seeds

1   teaspoon dry mustard

1   teaspoon ground turmeric

1 Prepare 5 (16-ounce) jars and lids for canning (page 9). Fill a canner halfway with water. Cover the canner and heat to simmering over High heat.

2 With a sharp knife, cut 8 cups kernels from corn cobs.

3 In a nonreactive 5-quart Dutch oven, combine corn, peppers, tomatoes, onions, sugar, vinegar, 4 teaspoons salt, celery seeds, dry mustard, and turmeric; heat to boiling over High heat. Reduce the heat; simmer, stirring, 20 minutes.

4 Ladle the simmering relish into hot jars to within ¼ inch of tops. (Keep the relish simmering while filling jars.) Wipe the jar rims and threads clean; cover quickly with lids and screw bands on securely but not too tightly. Process in a boiling-water bath (page 8) for 15 minutes; cool the jars and test for an airtight seal (page 10).

EACH SERVING (2 TABLESPOONS): ABOUT 15 CALORIES, 0G PROTEIN, 4G CARBOHYDRATES, 0G TOTAL FAT (0G SATURATED), 1G FIBER, 60MG SODIUM

QUICK
Sauerkraut

This fermented condiment is probiotic-rich and can aid in digestion.

ACTIVE TIME: 10 MINUTES **TOTAL TIME:** 10 MINUTES, PLUS COOLING **MAKES:** 1 (32-OUNCE) JAR

1¼ cups unseasoned rice vinegar

4 garlic cloves, crushed and peeled

3 tablespoons sugar

kosher salt

2 cups packed, thinly sliced cabbage

1 small onion, thinly sliced

4 star anises

2 teaspoons mustard seeds

1 In a small pot, combine rice vinegar, 1 cup water, garlic, sugar, and 2 tablespoons salt. Heat on Medium until sugar dissolves, stirring.

2 Arrange cabbage, onion, star anise, and mustard seeds in a 32-ounce jar; pour warm brine over cucumbers to cover. (Can be made in 2 or more smaller jars as long as there's enough brine to cover.) Let cool slightly.

3 Screw on the lid and refrigerate for at least 4 hours or up to 2 weeks.

EACH SERVING: ABOUT 10 CALORIES, 0G PROTEIN, 2G CARBOHYDRATE, 0G FAT (0G SATURATED), 0G FIBER, 323MG SODIUM

Pork & Sauerkraut STIR-FRY

This tangy stir-fry might rival your favorite takeout.

ACTIVE TIME: 5 MINUTES **TOTAL TIME:** 10 MINUTES **MAKES:** 4 SERVINGS

toasted sesame oil

1 pound ground pork

salt

1½ cups Quick Sauerkraut (prepared or above)

8 ounces shiitake mushrooms, stemmed and sliced

cooked rice, for serving

1 In a 12-inch skillet, heat 1 tablespoon oil on Medium-High. Add pork and ½ teaspoon salt; cook for 5 minutes, breaking up meat.

2 Add sauerkraut and mushrooms. Cook for 3 minutes, stirring. Serve with rice.

EACH SERVING: ABOUT 200 CALORIES, 25G PROTEIN, 7G CARBOHYDRATE, 8G FAT (2G SATURATED), 2G FIBER, 810MG SODIUM

Reuben
MACARONI AND CHEESE

If you're a fan of the sandwich, try out this mac 'n' cheese recipe that includes sauerkraut, Dijon mustard, and rye bread croutons.

ACTIVE TIME: 40 MINUTES **TOTAL TIME:** 50 MINUTES **MAKES:** 6 SERVINGS

1   pound elbow macaroni or other short pasta

2   tablespoons olive oil

1   medium onion, finely chopped

kosher salt

ground black pepper

1   clove garlic, crushed

1   tablespoon all-purpose flour

1½ cup whole milk

4   ounces low-fat cream cheese

3   tablespoon Dijon mustard

¼   teaspoon freshly grated or ground nutmeg

⅛   teaspoon cayenne

8   ounces extra-sharp Cheddar, shredded

8   ounces Gruyère, shredded

8   ounces Quick Sauerkraut (prepared or page 96), drained and squeezed of excess moisture

8   ounces deli corned beef, thinly sliced

4   slices rye bread, crust removed

1 Heat oven to 425°F. Oil a shallow 3-quart baking dish or six 2-cup ramekins. Cook the pasta according to package directions.

2 Meanwhile, heat 1 tablespoon of the oil in a large skillet over Medium-Low heat. Add the onion, ¾ teaspoon salt, and ¼ teaspoon pepper and cook, covered, stirring occasionally, until very tender, 8 to 10 minutes. Stir in the garlic and cook for 1 minute. Sprinkle the flour over the onion mixture and cook, stirring, for 1 minute.

3 Whisk in the milk and bring to a simmer. Whisk in the cream cheese, mustard, nutmeg, and cayenne until blended. Stir in the Cheddar and Gruyère and simmer, stirring occasionally, until cheese is melted and the mixture has slightly thickened, 1 to 2 minutes.

4 Toss the pasta with the cheese sauce, fold in the Quick Sauerkraut and corned beef, and transfer to the prepared baking dish. Tear the rye bread into ½-inch pieces. In a small bowl, toss together the rye bread pieces, remaining tablespoon oil, and ¼ teaspoon each salt and pepper. Sprinkle over the pasta mixture and bake until golden brown, 10 to 12 minutes.

EACH SERVING: ABOUT 630 CALORIES, 32G PROTEIN, 58G CARBOHYDRATE, 29G FAT (15G SATURATED), 4G FIBER, 1,213MG SODIUM

TIP

For a make-ahead meal, prepare the macaroni and cheese but do not bake. Cover and refrigerate for up to 2 days. Bake as directed, adding 15 to 20 minutes to the cooking time.

Quick Pickled
Red Onion
& Jalapeño
RELISH

In a medium bowl, whisk together **2 tablespoons lime juice**, **½ teaspoon honey**, **1 tablespoon olive oil**, and a **pinch each of kosher salt** and **ground black pepper**. Add **2 jalapeños**, chopped, **½ small red onion**, and **¼ cup cilantro**, roughly chopped; let sit, tossing occasionally, for at least 15 minutes and up to 1 hour. Makes 4 servings.

....

EACH SERVING: ABOUT 40 CALORIES, 0G PROTEIN, 2G CARBOHYDRATE, 3G FAT (0G SATURATED), 0G FIBER, 30MG SODIUM

Orange, Olive
& Sweet
Onion
RELISH

Cut away the peel and white pith of **2 oranges**. Working over a bowl, cut the orange into segments; the bowl will catch any juices. Cut the segments into ½-inch pieces. Add **¼ sweet onion**, chopped; **¼ cup small pitted green olives**, chopped; **¼ cup fresh flat-leaf parsley**, roughly chopped; **1 tablespoon olive oil**, and a **pinch each of kosher salt** and **ground black pepper** to the bowl, and gently toss to combine. Serve the relish with **4 large sweet or hot Italian sausages** and **rolls**. Makes 4 servings.

....

EACH SERVING: ABOUT 100 CALORIES, 1G PROTEIN, 10G CARBOHYDRATE, 5G FAT (1G SATURATED), 2G FIBER, 149MG SODIUM

Balsamic Tomatoes, Onion, Spinach & Blue Cheese
RELISH

In a medium bowl, whisk together **2 tablespoons olive oil**, **1 tablespoon balsamic vinegar**, and a **pinch each of kosher salt** and **ground black pepper**. Add **4 ounces grape tomatoes**, quartered, and **½ small red onion**, chopped, to the bowl and toss to combine. Fold in **1 cup spinach**, chopped, and then add **1 ounce crumbled blue cheese**. Makes 4 servings.

....

EACH SERVING: ABOUT 100 CALORIES, 2G PROTEIN, 3G CARBOHYDRATE, 9G FAT (2G SATURATED), 1G FIBER, 119MG SODIUM

Creamy Apple & Celery
RELISH

From 1 lemon, grate **1 teaspoon lemon zest** into a medium bowl. Squeeze in **1 tablespoon lemon juice**. Add **1 tablespoon mayonnaise**, 1 teaspoon whole-grain mustard, and a **pinch each of kosher salt** and **ground black pepper** to the bowl. Whisk together. Add **1 stalk celery**, chopped; **½ Granny Smith apple**, chopped; and **¼ cup fresh flat-leaf parsley**, roughly chopped, to the bowl and toss to combine. Makes 4 servings.

....

EACH SERVING: ABOUT 40 CALORIES, 0G PROTEIN, 4G CARBOHYDRATE, 3G FAT (0G SATURATED), 1G FIBER, 77MG SODIUM

Spicey Pickled Green Beans
(page 103)

5

Pickled Fruits & Vegetables

Once you've mastered the art of pickling, you can expand your skills to other vegetables and fruits. Green beans, okra, peaches, carrots, and onions can all make delicious pickles if you feel like branching out to other parts of the garden. Besides, these pickles make great additions to grilled meals, such as our Hoisin Chicken Burger with Pickled Red Onions. Be sure to pick produce that is ripe and also feels firm. Remove any bruises, blemishes, and stems before pickling and you will be good to go.

BONUS RECIPES

Italian Pickled Veggie Dip *(page 102),* **Spicy Tuna Sandwiches** *(page 103),* **Hoisin Chicken Burger with Pickled Red Onions** *(page 121)*

Giardiniera

This Italian pickled condiment gathers the best of the garden. Feel free to swap in another crunchy vegetable, like celery.

ACTIVE TIME: 10 MINUTES   **TOTAL TIME:** 10 MINUTES, PLUS COOLING   **MAKES:** 12 SERVINGS

1¼ cups distilled white vinegar

4   garlic cloves, crushed and peeled

3   tablespoons sugar

kosher salt

1   cup carrots, sliced

1   cup cauliflower florets

1   cup red peppers, chopped

2   sprigs rosemary

1 In a small pot, combine vinegar, 1 cup water, garlic, sugar, and 2 tablespoons salt. Heat on Medium until sugar dissolves, stirring.

2 Arrange carrots, cauliflower, peppers, and rosemary in a 32-ounce jar; pour warm brine over cucumbers to cover. (Can be made in two or more smaller jars as long as there's enough brine to cover.) Let cool slightly.

3 Screw on lid and refrigerate at least 1 day, or up to 2 weeks.

EACH SERVING: ABOUT 15 CALORIES, 0G PROTEIN, 3G CARBOHYDRATE, 0G FAT (0G SATURATED), 1G FIBER, 170MG SODIUM

Italian Pickled Veggie Dip

In food processor, pulse **4 ounces cream cheese**, softened; **½ cup plain Greek yogurt**; **½ cup chopped Giardiniera**; **2 green onions**, chopped; and **¼ teaspoon each of salt** and **pepper** just until combined, scraping bowl occasionally. Serve with crackers or crudités. Makes 8 servings.

EACH SERVING: ABOUT 70 CALORIES, 2G PROTEIN, 3G CARBOHYDRATE, 6G FAT (3G SATURATED), 0G FIBER, 155MG SODIUM

Spicy Pickled
GREEN BEANS

With fall comes a bounty of beautiful vegetables. To get the most out of them all year long, preserve your favorites, like these bright and fresh green beans, in a spicy brine.

ACTIVE TIME: 10 MINUTES   **TOTAL TIME:** 10 MINUTES   **MAKES:** 6 SERVINGS

4   cups leftover cooked green beans

5   garlic cloves, thinly sliced

2   teaspoons sugar

2   teaspoons salt

2   teaspoons peppercorns

2   dried red chili peppers

4   sprigs fresh dill

1   teaspoon coriander seeds

2   cups distilled white vinegar

1 Divide all the ingredients between two 16-ounce jars with lids.

2 Screw lids on jars to seal, and shake each for 1 minute. Refrigerate for at least 3 days before serving; pickled green beans will keep in the refrigerator for up to 1 week.

EACH SERVING: ABOUT 35 CALORIES, 2G PROTEIN, 8G CARBOHYDRATE, 0G FAT (0G SATURATED), 3G FIBER, 247MG SODIUM

Spicy Tuna Sandwiches

Combine **2 (5-ounce) cans tuna**, drained; ½ **cup mayonnaise**; ⅔ **cup chopped Spicy Pickled Green Beans**; **2 stalks celery**, finely chopped; **2 tablespoons Spicy Pickled Green Bean brine**; and **1 tablespoon snipped chives**. Serve on soft white bread. Makes 4 servings.

EACH SERVING: ABOUT 435 CALORIES, 20G PROTEIN, 35G CARBOHYDRATE, 24G FAT (4G SATURATED), 4G FIBER, 917MG SODIUM

PICKLED
Cauliflower

Chopped red pepper adds pops of color to this sweet pickled cauliflower.
The finished product will keep for up to a year in sealed jars.

ACTIVE TIME: 30 MINUTES   **TOTAL TIME:** 1 HOUR AND 5 MINUTES   **MAKES:** 6 (16-OUNCE) JARS

kosher salt

2   heads cauliflower, chopped

4   cups white vinegar

4   cups granulated sugar

1   medium onion

10   small sweet red cherry peppers

2   tablespoons yellow mustard seeds

1   tablespoon celery seeds

1   teaspoon ground turmeric

1   teaspoon red pepper flakes

1 Bring a large pot of water to a boil; salt the water (about 4 teaspoons salt per gallon of water). Boil the cauliflower for 3 minutes, then drain and run under cold water to cool. Divide among sterilized jars (2 cups per 16-ounce jar). Fill the pot with water again and bring to a boil.

2 In a large saucepan, combine the vinegar, sugar, onion, cherry peppers, mustard seeds, celery seeds, turmeric, pepper flakes, and 4 cups water. Bring to a boil, then reduce heat and simmer for 5 minutes.

3 Pour the vinegar mixture over the cauliflower in the jars, leaving a ½-inch space at the top; cover the jars. Working in batches, boil each jar for 15 minutes. Store the jars in a cool, dark place for at least 3 weeks, or for up to 1 year, before serving.

EACH SERVING: ABOUT 15 CALORIES, 1G PROTEIN, 3G CARBOHYDRATE, 0G FAT (0G SATURATED), 1G FIBER, 133MG SODIUM

PICKLED
Beets

Delicious beets for your summer cookout!

ACTIVE TIME: 15 MINUTES   **TOTAL TIME:** 35 MINUTES, PLUS CHILLING   **MAKES:** 8 SERVINGS

coarse salt

2   pounds medium golden, red, or striped beets

1¼   cups cider vinegar

⅓   cup sugar

4   pieces orange peel

½   teaspoon whole black peppercorns

¼   teaspoon allspice berries

2   whole cloves

1   stick cinnamon

1 Bring a large saucepan of water to boil over High heat. Add 2 teaspoons salt and the beets and cook until just tender, about 30 minutes. Drain and rinse the beets under cold water. Set aside to cool.

2 Bring the remaining ingredients, 1 teaspoon salt, and 1½ cups water to a boil over High heat in a medium saucepan. Reduce the heat to Low and simmer for 5 minutes. Peel the beets, slice into ¼-inch-thick rounds, and place in a medium bowl with the simmered liquid. Cool to room temperature.

3 Cover and marinate in the fridge overnight or for up to 24 hours. Store beets in an airtight container for up to 2 weeks.

EACH SERVING: ABOUT 45 CALORIES, 1G PROTEIN, 10G CARBOHYDRATE, 0G FAT (0G SATURATED), 2G FIBER, 246MG SODIUM

PICKLED
Okra

Tender okra pods preserved with dill, garlic, and crushed red pepper are an old-time Southern favorite.

ACTIVE TIME: 20 MINUTES   **TOTAL TIME:** 20 MINUTES, PLUS PROCESSING   **MAKES:** 8 (8-OUNCE) JARS

3½ cups distilled white vinegar

kosher, canning, or pickling salt

8   garlic cloves, peeled

8   dill sprigs

2   teaspoons crushed red pepper

1¼ pounds small firm okra, stems trimmed

1 Prepare 8 (8-ounce) jars and lids (page 9). Fill canner halfway with water, cover and heat to simmering over High heat.

2 In nonreactive 2-quart saucepan, combine vinegar, 2 cups water, and ¼ cup salt; heat to boiling over High heat.

3 In each hot jar, place 1 garlic clove, 1 dill sprig, and ¼ teaspoon crushed red pepper. Tightly pack okra, stem end up, into hot jars. Immediately ladle simmering liquid over okra to within ¼ inch of tops, making sure okra is completely covered with liquid. (Keep liquid simmering while filling jars.) Wipe jar rims and threads clean; cover with lids, and screw band on securely but not too tightly. Process in boiling-water bath (page 8) for 10 minutes; cool jars and test for airtight seal (page 10).

EACH (2-OUNCE) SERVING: ABOUT 10 CALORIES, 0G PROTEIN, 3G CARBOHYDRATE, 0G FAT (0G SATURATED), 1G FIBER, 874MG SODIUM

PICKLED
Radishes

Radishes stand up against a vinegar brine and will retain crunch, too. Serve them with fish tacos, spicy curries, and roast beef sandwiches.

ACTIVE TIME: 10 MINUTES   **TOTAL TIME:** 10 MINUTES   **MAKES:** 6 SERVINGS

1½ cups rice vinegar

½ cup honey

1 stalk lemongrass

2 teaspoons fresh ginger, peeled and minced

1 teaspoon mustard seeds

2 cups radishes

1 In a small pot, bring vinegar, honey, lemongrass, ginger, mustard seeds, and ¼ cup water to a boil. Remove from heat and let cool to room temperature, about 1 hour.

2 Strain pickling liquid into heatproof canning jars, or a bowl, and discard solids. Add radishes. Seal jars, or cover bowl, and refrigerate overnight before serving. Radishes will keep, refrigerated, for up to 3 days.

EACH SERVING: ABOUT 15 CALORIES, 0G PROTEIN, 4G CARBOHYDRATE, 0G FAT (0G SATURATED), 1G FIBER, 15MG SODIUM

PICKLED
Roasted Peppers

These pickled red and yellow peppers are
fun and tasty on a sandwich, too.

ACTIVE TIME: 20 MINUTES   **TOTAL TIME:** 1 HOUR AND 20 MINUTES   **MAKES:** 13 SERVINGS

2   medium red peppers

2   medium yellow peppers

canola oil

kosher salt

ground black pepper

½   cup white wine vinegar

½   cup cider vinegar

1   garlic clove

2   tablespoons sugar

2   tablespoons finely chopped fresh
     oregano leaves

1 Preheat your oven to 400°F. On a jelly-roll pan,
brush red and yellow peppers with 2 teaspoons
oil and sprinkle with ¼ teaspoon salt and
⅛ teaspoon pepper. Roast 30 minutes or until
charred on all sides, turning occasionally.
Transfer to bowl, cover with plastic wrap,
and let stand 15 minutes.

2 Meanwhile, in a 1½-quart saucepan,
combine vinegars, ½ cup water, garlic, sugar,
and 1 tablespoon salt. Heat to boiling on High,
stirring. Boil 1 minute. Remove from heat;
let cool.

3 Peel off skin from peppers and discard; remove
and discard stems and seeds. Thinly slice peppers
and transfer to medium bowl.

4 Stir in oregano and vinegar mixture. Cover
and refrigerate for at least 4 hours, or up to
2 days.

EACH SERVING: ABOUT 20 CALORIES, 1G PROTEIN,
4G CARBOHYDRATE, 0G FAT (0G SATURATED),
0G FIBER, 112MG SODIUM

PICKLED
Sour Cherries

Pair this garnish with cheeses, salads, cocktails,
or any favorite summer recipe.

ACTIVE TIME: 5 MINUTES   **TOTAL TIME:** 15 MINUTES   **MAKES:** 8 SERVINGS

⅛   cup rice vinegar

1¼   cups sugar

1   slice fresh ginger, peeled

15   black peppercorns

kosher salt

1⅓   pounds fresh sour cherries

1 In a medium nonreactive pan, bring vinegar, sugar, ginger, peppercorns, and ½ teaspoon salt to a boil. Set aside.

2 Pack cherries into a heatproof jar. Pour hot vinegar mixture over cherries until covered. Let cool completely. Seal jar and refrigerate cherries for at least 1 day before serving. Cherries will keep, refrigerated, up to 8 weeks. Serve cherries as a garnish in a cocktail, or accompanying a salad or cheese plate.

EACH SERVING: ABOUT 85 CALORIES, 1G PROTEIN,
21G CARBOHYDRATE, 0G FAT (0G SATURATED),
1G FIBER, 17MG SODIUM

Peaches with Pepper

Pinot grigio vinegar gives this dessert a light and delicate flavor.

ACTIVE TIME: 10 MINUTES   **TOTAL TIME:** 1 HOUR AND 10 MINUTES   **MAKES:** 2 SERVINGS

¼   cup Pinot Grigio vinegar

¼   cup sugar

2   ripe peaches

¼   teaspoon tricolor peppercorns

1 Combine the vinegar and sugar in a medium bowl and stir to dissolve sugar.

2 Add the peaches to the vinegar mixture, sprinkle with the peppercorns, and toss gently to combine.

3 Chill for 30 minutes to 1 hour in the refrigerator. Serve with lemon sorbet, if desired.

EACH SERVING: ABOUT 160 CALORIES, 1G PROTEIN, 21G CARBOHYDRATE, 0G FAT (0G SATURATED), 2G FIBER, 1MG SODIUM

TIP

Look for Pinot Grigio vinegar in specialty stores and supermarkets, or substitute another white wine vinegar.

PICKLED
Plums

This refreshing preserved fruit is flavored with a mix of spices, including mustard seed, caraway seed, coriander, and cloves. Serve with cheese or roasted pork or chicken.

ACTIVE TIME: 15 MINUTES   **TOTAL TIME:** 2 HOURS   **MAKES:** 12 SERVINGS

½   large yellow onion

½   teaspoon fennel seed

1   teaspoon yellow mustard seed

½   teaspoon caraway seed

½   teaspoon coriander

2   whole cloves

salt

¼   cup sugar

1   cup distilled vinegar

1   cup mirin

1   pound small plums, sliced

1 Combine the onion, fennel seed, mustard seed, caraway seed, coriander, cloves, 4 teaspoons salt, sugar, vinegar, and mirin in a medium saucepan, and bring to a boil over Medium-High heat.
2 Reduce the heat to Medium-Low, and simmer until the sugar is dissolved. Remove from heat.
3 Separate the sliced plums into airtight containers. Pour the liquid from steps 1 and 2 over the plums.
4 Chill uncovered for 2 hours before serving. Cover once the liquid is chilled, and store refrigerated for up to 2 weeks.

EACH SERVING: ABOUT 30 CALORIES, 0G PROTEIN, 6G CARBOHYDRATE, 0G FAT (0G SATURATED), 1G FIBER, 164MG SODIUM

TIP
Mirin, or Japanese sweet rice wine, adds subtle flavor to dishes. Find it in the Asian foods section of most grocery stores. If you can't find it, dissolve ¼ cup sugar in 1 cup vermouth as a substitute.

PICKLED
Red Onions

The sweet and pungent flavor of red onions balances well
with tangy white vinegar in this pickled treat.

ACTIVE TIME: 15 MINUTES   **TOTAL TIME:** 20 MINUTES   **MAKES:** 3/4 CUP

1   red onion, thinly sliced (about 1 cup)

⅓   cup fresh lime juice

¼   cup distilled white vinegar

kosher salt

1 In a small bowl, combine sliced onion, lime juice, vinegar, and 1 teaspoon kosher salt.

2 Cover the bowl and place it in the refrigerator for at least 20 minutes, stirring occasionally.

3 After 20 minutes, transfer the onions and vinegar mixture to a jar. Refrigerate until ready to use or up to 2 weeks.

EACH SERVING: ABOUT 20 CALORIES, 0G PROTEIN, 4G CARBOHYDRATE, 0G FAT (0G SATURATED), 1G FIBER, 2G SODIUM

Safety in the Pantry

Before eating canned food, check the jar carefully for signs of spoilage.

DO NOT TASTE OR USE ANY CANNED FOOD IF the lid is loose; there are gas bubbles; there is spurting liquid; the contents are moldy, slimy, or uncharacteristically soft or mushy; the color is unnatural; there is sediment at the bottom of the jar; or the food smells unpleasant.

If you reject the contents of a jar, destroy the food in such a way that it cannot be accidentally eaten by children or pets. Be sure to wear heavy plastic gloves when you handle it, as botulinum toxins can be fatal when ingested or absorbed through the skin. Afterward, thoroughly wash any surface that may have come in contact with the spoiled food using a chlorine solution, and discard any kitchen sponges used during cleanup.

Hoisin Chicken Burger
WITH PICKLED RED ONIONS

Tart, tangy, and sweet, pickled red onions and Chinese hoisin sauce make a surprisingly flavorful but simple topping for lean chicken burgers.

ACTIVE TIME: 25 MINUTES **TOTAL TIME:** 45 MINUTES **MAKES:** 4 SERVINGS

HOISIN SAUCE

½ cup rice vinegar

kosher salt

1 tablespoon sugar

½ star anise

8 peppercorns

½ red onion, sliced into rings

PICKLED RED ONIONS & CHICKEN BURGER

¼ cup minced red onion

1 pound ground chicken

¼ cup minced red bell pepper

2 garlic cloves, crushed

6 tablespoons prepared hoisin sauce

2 tablespoons breadcrumbs

2 tablespoons sesame seeds

1 tablespoon grated ginger

4 teaspoons soy sauce

olive oil

4 sesame-seed buns

lettuce (for serving)

1 To prepare the Sauce: In a small saucepan over Medium heat, combine the rice vinegar, 1½ teaspoons kosher salt, sugar, star anise, and peppercorns; bring to a gentle simmer. Remove pan from heat and let cool to room temperature. Add onion rings and stir; let steep.

2 To prepare the Onions & Burger: Preheat your grill to Medium-High heat. Meanwhile, in a large bowl, combine minced onion, chicken, bell pepper, garlic, 4 tablespoons hoisin sauce, breadcrumbs, sesame seeds, ginger, and soy sauce. Form the mixture into 4 patties.

3 Brush the grate with oil, and grill burgers for about 4 minutes; flip and repeat, brushing with remaining hoisin sauce during the last minute. Meanwhile, strain and reserve pickled onions, discarding the liquid. Assemble burgers on buns with lettuce and reserved pickled onions.

EACH SERVING: ABOUT 420 CALORIES, 23G PROTEIN, 45G CARBOHYDRATE, 15G FAT (4G SATURATED), 4G FIBER, 1,094MG SODIUM

PICKLED
Heirloom Carrots

Quick and simple, these sweet heirloom carrots pickled in a tangy, spice-laden brine make a great addition to any dish.

ACTIVE TIME: 10 MINUTES   **TOTAL TIME:** 25 MINUTES   **MAKES:** 10 SERVINGS

1   pound small carrots (such as orange, white, and red)

1½ cups cider vinegar

⅓   cup honey

salt

¾   tablespoon mustard seeds

¾   tablespoon fennel seeds

¾   tablespoon black peppercorns

¾   tablespoon crushed coriander seeds

1   dried hot chili pepper

1 Bring a large pot of water to a boil; blanch carrots for 2 minutes. Drain and shock in a large bowl of cold water. Drain and set aside.

2 In a medium pan, bring 1 cup water, vinegar, honey, and 2 tablespoons salt to a boil.

3 Meanwhile, pack a sterilized 1-quart Mason jar with carrots. Remove pan from heat and add remaining ingredients, stirring to combine. Ladle hot brine over carrots until just covered. Seal the jar and refrigerate carrots overnight.

EACH SERVING: ABOUT 25 CALORIES, 1G PROTEIN, 6G CARBOHYDRATE, 0G FAT (0G SATURATED), 1G FIBER, 226MG SODIUM

PICKLED
Zucchini

Sometimes bigger isn't better. Look for smaller zucchinis
with rich, vibrant coloring for best pick of the produce.

ACTIVE TIME: 15 MINUTES   **TOTAL TIME:** 15 MINUTES, PLUS PICKLING   **MAKES:** 8 SERVINGS

2   cups sugar

2   cups distilled white vinegar

2   tablespoons pickling spice

4   bay leaves

1   large onion, thinly sliced

4   medium zucchini, cut in 1-inch chunks

1 In a 2-quart saucepan over High heat, heat sugar, vinegar, pickling spice, and bay leaves to boiling. Add sliced onion; cook for 1 minute.

2 Place zucchini in an 11 x 7-inch glass baking dish. Pour the vinegar mixture over zucchini. Cover with plastic wrap and refrigerate overnight to allow flavors to develop, stirring occasionally. Drain before serving. Serve with grilled steak, chicken, or hamburgers. If you like, store in decorative jars in the refrigerator.

EACH SERVING: ABOUT 50 CALORIES, 1G PROTEIN, 11G CARBOHYDRATE, 0G FAT (0G SATURATED), 1G FIBER, 8MG SODIUM

Index

Photo Credits

Metric Conversion Charts

The recipes that appear in this cookbook use the standard United States method for measuring liquid and dry or solid ingredients (teaspoons, tablespoons, and cups). The information on this chart is provided to help cooks outside the U.S. successfully use these recipes. All equivalents are approximate.

METRIC EQUIVALENTS FOR DIFFERENT TYPES OF INGREDIENTS

STANDARD CUP (e.g., flour)	FINE POWDER (e.g., rice)	GRAIN (e.g., sugar)	GRANULAR (e.g., butter)	LIQUID SOLIDS (e.g., milk)	LIQUID
¾	105 g	113 g	143 g	150 g	180 ml
⅔	93 g	100 g	125 g	133 g	160 ml
½	70 g	75 g	95 g	100 g	120 ml
⅓	47 g	50 g	63 g	67 g	80 ml
¼	35 g	38 g	48 g	50 g	60 ml
⅛	18 g	19 g	24 g	25 g	30 ml

USEFUL EQUIVALENTS FOR LIQUID INGREDIENTS BY VOLUME

¼ tsp	=					1 ml
½ tsp	=					2 ml
1 tsp	=					5 ml
3 tsp	=	1 tbsp	=	½ fl oz	=	15 ml
		2 tbsp	=	⅛ cup	=	1 fl oz	=	30 ml
		4 tbsp	=	¼ cup	=	2 fl oz	=	60 ml
		5⅓ tbsp	=	⅓ cup	=	3 fl oz	=	80 ml
		8 tbsp	=	½ cup	=	4 fl oz	=	120 ml
		10⅔ tbsp	=	⅔ cup	=	5 fl oz	=	160 ml
		12 tbsp	=	¾ cup	=	6 fl oz	=	180 ml
		16 tbsp	=	1 cup	=	8 fl oz	=	240 ml
		1 pt	=	2 cups	=	16 fl oz	=	480 ml
		1 qt	=	4 cups	=	32 fl oz	=	960 ml
					33 fl oz	=	1000 ml = 1 L

USEFUL EQUIVALENTS FOR DRY INGREDIENTS BY WEIGHT

(To convert ounces to grams, multiply the number of ounces by 30.)

1 oz	=	¹⁄₁₆ lb	=	30 g
2 oz	=	¼ lb	=	120 g
4 oz	=	½ lb	=	240 g
8 oz	=	¾ lb	=	360 g
16 oz	=	1 lb	=	480 g

USEFUL EQUIVALENTS FOR COOKING/OVEN TEMPERATURES

	Fahrenheit	Celsius	Gas Mark
Freeze Water	32°F	0°C	
Room Temperature	68°F	20°C	
Boil Water	212°F	100°C	
Bake	325°F	160°C	3
	350°F	180°C	4
	375°F	190°C	5
	400°F	200°C	6
	425°F	220°C	7
	450°F	230°C	8
Broil			Grill

USEFUL EQUIVALENTS LENGTH

(To convert inches to centimeters, multiply the number of inches by 2.5.)

1 in	=					2.5 cm
6 in	=	½ ft	=			15 cm
12 in	=	1 ft	=			30 cm
36 in	=	3 ft	=	1 yd	=	90 cm
40 in	=					100 cm	=	1 m

THE GOOD HOUSEKEEPING
TRIPLE-TEST PROMISE

At *Good Housekeeping*, we want to make sure that every recipe we print works in any oven, with any brand of ingredient, no matter what. That's why, in our test kitchens at the **Good Housekeeping Research Institute**, we go all out: We test each recipe at least three times—and, often, several more times after that.

When a recipe is first developed, one member of our team prepares the dish, and we judge it on these criteria: It must be **delicious**, **family-friendly**, **healthful**, and **easy to make**.

1 The recipe is then tested several more times to fine-tune the flavor and ease of preparation, always by the same team member, using the same equipment.

2 Next, another team member follows the recipe as written, **varying the brands of ingredients** and **kinds of equipment**. Even the types of stoves we use are changed.

3 A third team member repeats the whole process **using yet another set of equipment** and **alternative ingredients**. By the time the recipes appear on these pages, they are guaranteed to work in any kitchen, including yours. **We promise.**